THE LITERARY DOG

THE LITERARY DOG

EDITED BY
William E. Maloney
Jean-Claude Suarès

DESIGNED BY
Seymour Chwast
Richard Mantel

A Push Pin Press Book

Berkley Windhover Books

 PUSH PIN PRESS

Producer: Jean-Claude Suarès
Editorial Director: William E. Maloney
Design Director: Seymour Chwast

Produced by Push Pin Press
for Berkley Windhover Books

SBN: 425-03961-7 (paper)
SBN: 399-12301-6 (cloth)
Library of Congress Catalog
Card Number: 78-14536

BERKLEY WINDHOVER BOOKS
are published by Berkley Publishing
Corporation, 200 Madison Avenue,
New York, N.Y. 10016.

Printed in the United States of America.

Berkley Windhover Edition, October, 1978.

The great pleasure of a dog is that you may make a fool of yourself with him and not only will he not scold you, but he will make a fool of himself too.

Samuel Butler

Contents

Konrad Lorenz

1903-

MAN MEETS DOG
Excerpt

I once possessed a fascinating little book of crazy tales called 'Snowshoe Al's Bedtime Stories'. It concealed behind a mask of ridiculous nonsense that penetrating and somewhat cruel satire which is one of the characteristic features of American humour, and which is not always easily intelligible to many Europeans. In one of these stories Snowshoe Al relates with romantic sentimentality the heroic deeds of his best friend. Incidents of incredible courage, exaggerated manliness and complete altruism are piled up in a comical parody of Western American romanticism culminating in the touching scenes where the hero saves his friend's life from wolves, grizzly bears, hunger, cold and all the manifold dangers which beset him. The story ends with the laconic statement, 'In so doing, his feet became so badly frozen that I unfortunately had to shoot him.'

If I ask a man who has just been boasting of the prowess and other wonderful properties of one of his dogs, I always ask him whether he has still got the animal. The answer, then, is all too often strongly reminiscent of Snowshoe Al's story, "No, I had to get rid of him—I moved to another town —or into a smaller house—I got another job and it was awkward for me to keep a dog," or some other similar excuse. It is to me amazing that many people who are otherwise morally sound feel no disgrace in admitting such an action. They do not realize that there is no difference between their behaviour and that of the satirized egoist in the story. The animal is deprived of rights, not only by the letter of the law, but also by many people's insensitivity.

The fidelity of a dog is a precious gift demanding no less binding moral responsibilities than the friendship of a human being. The bond with a true dog is as lasting as the ties of this earth can ever be, a fact which should be noted by anyone who decides to acquire a canine friend. It may of course happen that the love of a dog is thrust upon one involuntarily, a circumstance which occurred to me when I met the Hanoverian Schweisshund, 'Hirschmann', on a ski-ing tour. He was at the time about a year old and a typical masterless dog; for his owner the head forester only loved his old Deutscher Rauhaar (German Pointer) and had no time for the clumsy stripling which showed few signs of ever becoming a gun-dog. Hirschmann was soft and sensi-

tive and a little shy of his master, a fact which did not speak highly for the training ability of the forester. On the other hand I did not think any the better of the dog for coming out with us as early as the second day of our stay. I took him for a sycophant, quite wrongly as it turned out, for he was following not us but me alone. When one morning I found him sleeping outside by bedroom door, I began to reconsider my first opinion and to suspect that a great canine love was germinating. I realized it too late: the oath of allegiance had been sworn nor would the dog recant on the day of my departure. I tried to catch him in order to shut him up and prevent from following us, but he refused to come near me. Quivering with consternation and with his tail between his legs he stood at a safe distance saying with his eyes, 'I'll do anything at all for you—except leave you!' I capitulated. 'Forester, what's the price of your dog?' The forester, from whose point of view the dog's conduct was sheer desertion, replied without a moment's consideration, 'Ten shillings.' It sounded like an expletive and was meant as such. Before he could think of a better one, the ten shillings were in his hand and two pairs of skis and two pairs of dog's paws were under way. I knew that Hirschmann would follow us but surmised erroneously that, plagued by his conscience, he would slink after us at a distance, thinking that he was not allowed to come with us. What really did happen was entirely unexpected. The full weight of the huge dog hit me broadsides on like a cannon ball and I was precipitated hip foremost on to the icy road. A skier's equilibrium is not proof against the impact of an enormous dog, hurled in a delirium of excitement against him. I had quite underestimated his grasp of the situation. As for Hirschmann, he danced for joy over my extended corpse.

I have always taken very seriously the responsibility imposed by a dog's fidelity, and I am proud that I once risked my life, though inadvertently, to save a dog which had fallen into the Danube at a temperature of $-28°$ C. My Alsatian, Bingo, was running along the frozen edge of the river when he slipped and fell into the water. His claws were unable to grip the sides of the ice so he could not get out. Dogs become exhausted very quickly when attempting to get up too steep a bank. They get into an awkward, more and more upright swimming position until they are soon in imminent danger of drowning. I therefore ran a few yards ahead of the dog which was being swept downstream; then I lay down and, in order to distribute my weight, crept on my belly to the edge of the ice. As Bingo came within my reach, I seized him by the scruff of the neck and pulled him with a jerk towards me on to the ice, but our joint weight was too much for it—it broke, and I slid silently, head first into the freezing cold water. The dog, which, unlike myself, had its head shorewards, managed to reach firmer ice. Now the situation was reversed; Bingo ran apprehensively along the ice and I floated downstream in the current. Finally, because the human hand is better adapted than the paw of the dog for gripping a smooth surface, I managed to escape disaster by my own efforts. I felt ground beneath my feet and threw my upper half upon the ice.

We judge the moral worth of two human friends according to which of them is ready to make the greater sacrifice without thought of recompense. Nietzsche who, unlike most people, wore brutality only as a mask to hide true warmness of heart, said the beautiful words, 'Let it be your aim always to love more than the other, never to be the second.' With human beings, I am sometimes able to fulfil this commandment, but in my relations with a faithful dog, I am always the second. What a strange and unique social relationship! Have you ever thought how extraordinary it all is? Man, endowed with reason and a highly developed sense of moral responsibility, whose finest and noblest belief is the religion of brotherly love, in this very respect falls short of the carnivores. In saying this I am not indulging in sentimental anthropomorphization. Even the noblest human love arises, not from reason and the specifically human, rational moral sense, but from the much deeper age-old layers of instinctive feeling. The highest and most selfless moral behaviour loses all value in our estimation when it arises not from such sources but from the reason. Elizabeth Browning said,

If thou must love me, let it be for nought
Except for love's sake only.

Even to-day man's heart is still the same as that of the higher social animals, no matter how far the achievements of his reason and his rational moral sense transcend theirs. The plain fact that my dog loves me more than I love him is undeniable and always fills me with a certain feeling of shame. The dog is ever ready to lay down his life for me. If a lion or a tiger threatened me, Ali, Bully, Tito, Stasi, and all the others would, without a moment's hesitation, have plunged into the hopeless fight to protect my life if only for a few seconds. And I?

If you pick up a starving dog and make him prosperous, he will not bite you. This is the principal difference between a dog and a man.

Mark Twain

Homer

Sixth Century B.C.

THE ODYSSEY

Thus, near the gates conferring as they drew,
Argus, the dog, his ancient master knew;
He, not unconscious of the voice and tread,
Lifts to the sound his ear, and rears his head;
Bred by Ulysses, nourished at his board,
But ah! not fated long to please his lord,
To him, his swiftness and his strength were vain;
The voice of glory called him o'er the main.

Till then in every sylvan chase renown'd,
With Argus, Argus, rang the woods around;
With him pursued the youth the goat or fawn,
Or traced the mazy leveret o'er the lawn;
Now left to man's ingratitude he lay,

Unhoused, neglected in the public way.
He knew his lord—he knew, and strove to meet.
In vain he strove to crawl, and kiss his feet;
Yet (all he could) his tail, his ears, his eyes,
Salute his master and confess his joys.
Soft pity touch'd the mighty master's soul,
Adown his cheek a tear unbidden stole.

The dog whom Fate had granted to behold
His lord, when twenty tedious years had roll'd,
Takes a last look, and, having seen him, dies;
So closed forever faithful Argus' eyes.

Juliana Berners

Fifteenth Century

THE GREYHOUNDE

A greyhounde should be headed lyke a snake,
And neckyd lyke a drake,
Fotyd lyke a cat,
Tayled lyke a ratte,
Syded lyke a teme,
And chyned lyke a bream,
The fyrste yere he must lerne to fede,
The seconde yere to feld him lede.
The thyrde yere he is felow lyke.
The fourth yere there is non syke.
The fifth yere he is good ynough.
The syxth yere he shall hold the plough,
The seventh yere he will avaylle
Grete bytches for assayle.
But when he is come to the ninth yere
Have him then to the tannere.
For the best hounde that ever bytch had
At the ninth yere is full bad.

11

William Cowper

1731-1800

ON A SPANIEL CALLED BEAU
KILLING A YOUNG BIRD

A Spaniel, Beau, that fares like you,
Well-fed, and at his ease,
Should wiser be, than to pursue
Each trifle that he sees.

But you have kill'd a tiny bird,
Which flew not till to-day,
Against my orders, whom you heard
Forbidding you the prey.

Nor did you kill, that you might eat,
And ease a doggish pain,
For him, though chas'd with furious heat,
You left where he was slain.

Nor was he of the thievish sort,
Or one whom blood allures,
But innocent was all his sport,
Whom you have torn for yours.

My dog! what remedy remains,
Since, teach you all I can,
I see you, after all my pains,
So much resemble man!

BEAU'S REPLY

Sir! when I flew to seize the bird,
In spite of your command,
A louder voice than yours I heard
And harder to withstand:

You cried—Forbear!—but in my breast
A mightier cried—Proceed!
'Twas nature, Sir, whose strong behest
Impell'd me to the deed.

Yet much as nature I respect,
I ventur'd once to break
(As you perhaps may recollect)
Her precept, for your sake;

And when your linnet, on a day,
Passing his prison-door,
Had flutter'd all his strength away,
And panting press'd the floor,

Well knowing him a sacred thing,
Not destin'd to my tooth,
I only kiss'd his ruffled wing,
And lick'd the feathers smooth.

Let my obedience then excuse
My disobedience now,
Nor some reproof yourself refuse
From your aggriev'd Bow-wow!

If killing birds be such a crime,
(Which I can hardly see)
What think you, Sir, of killing Time
With verse address'd to me?

FOP

Though once a puppy, and though Fop by name,
Here moulders One whose bones some honour claim.
No sycophant, although of spaniel race,
And though no hound, a martyr to the chase.
Ye squirrels, rabbits, leverets, rejoice,
Your haunts no longer echo to his voice;
This record of his fate exulting view,
He died worn out with vain pursuit of you.
'Yes,' the indignant shade of Fop replies—
'And worn with vain pursuit Man also dies.'

Lord Byron

1788-1824

EPITAPH TO A
NEWFOUNDLAND DOG

Near this spot
Are deposited the Remains of one
Who possessed Beauty without Vanity,
Strength without Insolence,
Courage without Ferocity,
And all the Virtues of Man, without his Vices.
This Praise, which would be unmeaning Flattery
If inscribed over human ashes,
Is but a just Tribute to the Memory of
BOATSWAIN, a Dog,
Who was born at Newfoundland, May, 1803,
And died at Newstead Abbey, Nov. 18, 1808.

The dogs eat of the crumbs which fall from their
masters' table.   *Matthew XIII. 32*

A NEWFOUNDLAND

His hair, his size, his mouth, his lugs,
Show'd he was nane o' Scotland's dogs;
But whalpit some place far abroad,
Where sailors gang to fish for cod.

Robert Burns

12

William Robert Spencer

1769-1834

BETH-GÊLERT

The spearmen heard the bugle sound,
And cheerily smiled the morn;
And many a brach, and many a hound
Obeyed Llewellyn's horn.

And still he blew a louder blast,
And gave a lustier cheer,
"Come, Gêlert, come, wert never last
Llewellyn's horn to hear.

"O where does faithful Gelert roam
The flower of all his race;
So true, so brave—a lamb at home,
A lion in the chase?"

In sooth, he was a peerless hound,
The gift of royal John;
But now no Gêlert could be found,
And all the chase rode on.

That day Llewellyn little loved
The chase of hart and hare;
And scant and small the booty proved,
For Gêlert was not there.

Unpleased, Llewellyn homeward hied,
When, near the portal seat,
His truant Gêlert he espied
Bounding his lord to greet.

But when he gained the castle-door,
Aghast the chieftain stood;
The hound all o'er was smeared with gore;
His lips, his fangs, ran blood.

Llewellyn gazed with fierce surprise;
Unused such looks to meet,
His favorite checked his joyful guise,
And crouched, and licked his feet.

Onward, in haste, Llewellyn passed,
And on went Gêlert too;
And still, where'er his eyes he cast,
Fresh blood-gouts shocked his view.

O'erturned his infant's bed he found,
With blood-stained covert rent;
And all around the walls and ground
With recent blood besprent.

He called his child—no voice replied—
He searched with terror wild;
Blood, blood he found on every side,
But nowhere found his child.

"Hell-hound! my child's by thee devoured,"
The frantic father cried;
And to the hilt his vengeful sword
He plunged in Gelert's side.

Aroused by Gelert's dying yell,
Some slumberer wakened nigh;
What words the parent's joy could tell
To hear his infant's cry!

Concealed beneath a tumbled heap
His hurried search had missed
All glowing from his rosy sleep
The cherub boy he kissed.

Nor scathe had he, nor harm, nor dread,
But, the same couch beneath,
Lay a gaunt wolf, all torn and dead,
Tremendous still in death.

Ah, what was then Llewellyn's pain!
For now the truth was clear;
His gallant hound the wolf had slain.
To save Llewellyn's heir.

Sir, a woman's preaching is like a dog's walking on his hinder legs. It is not done well, but you are surprised to find it done at all.

Samuel Johnson

William Shakespeare

1564-1616

MIDSUMMER NIGHT'S DREAM

My hounds are bred out of the Spartan kind,
So flewed, so sanded; and their heads are hung
With ears that sweep away the morning dew;
Crook-kneed, and dew-lapped like Thessalian bulls,
Slow in pursuit, but matched in mouth like bells,
Each unto each. A cry more tunable
Was never hollaed to, nor cheered with horn,
In Crete, in Sparta, nor in Thessaly:
Judge when you hear.

THE TWO GENTLEMEN OF VERONA

Enter Launce with his dog

LAUNCE: When a man's servant shall play the cur with him, look you, it goes hard: one that I brought up of a puppy; one that I saved from drowning, when three of four of his blind brothers and sisters went to it. I have taught him, even as one would say precisely, 'Thus I would teach a dog'. I was sent to deliver him as a present to Mistress Silvia from my master, and I came no sooner into the dining chamber but he steps me to her trencher and steals her capon's leg. O! 'tis a foul thing when a cur cannot keep himself in all companies. I would have, as one should say, one that takes upon him to be a dog indeed, to be, as it were, a dog at all things. If I had not more wit than he, to take a fault upon me that he did, I think verily he had been hanged for't: sure as I live, he had suffered for't: you shall judge. He thrusts himself into the company of three or four gentlemanlike dogs under the duke's table: he had not been there—bless the mark!—a pissing-while, but all the chamber smelt him. 'Out with dog!' says one; 'What cur is that?' says another. 'Whip him out', says the third; 'Hang him up', says the duke. I, having been acquainted with the smell before, knew it was Crab, and goes me to the fellow that whips the dogs. 'Friend', quoth I, 'you mean to whip the dog?' 'Ay, marry, do I', quoth he. 'You do him the more wrong', quoth I: 'twas I did the thing you wot of'. He makes me no more ado, but whips me out of the chamber. How many masters would do this for his servant? Nay, I'll be sworn, I have sat in the stocks for puddings he hath stolen, otherwise he had been executed: I have stood on the pillory for geese he hath killed, otherwise he had suffered for't; thou thinkest not of this now. Nay, I remember the trick you served me when I took leave of Madam Silvia: did not I bid thee still mark me and do as I do? When didst thou see me heave up my leg and make water against a gentlewoman's farthingale? Didst thou ever see me do such a trick?

I am his Highness' dog at Kew;
Pray tell me, sir, whose dog are you?
*Inscription on collar of dog
given by Alexander Pope to his Royal Highness*

At night my wife and I did fall out about the dog's being put down in the cellar, which I had a mind to have done because of his fouling the house, and I would have my will; and so we went to bed and lay all night in a quarrel.   *Samuel Pepys*

FOOT-WARMERS

The churches were all unheated. Few had stoves until the middle of this century. The chill of the damp buildings, never heated from autumn to spring, and closed and dark throughout the week, was hard for every one to bear. In some of the early log-built meeting-houses, fur bags made of wolfskins were nailed to the seats; and in winter church attendants thrust their feet into them. Dogs, too, were permitted to enter the meeting-house and lie on their masters' feet. Dog-whippers or dog-pelters were appointed to control and expel them when they became unruly or unbearable.

Home Life in Colonial Days

Oliver Goldsmith

1730-1774

ELEGY ON THE DEATH OF A MAD DOG

Good people all, of every sort,
Give ear unto my song;
And if you find it wondrous short,
It cannot hold you long.

In Islington there was a man,
Of whom the world might say,
That still a godly race he ran,
Whene'er he went to pray.

A kind and gentle heart he had,
To comfort friends and foes;
The naked every day he clad,
When he put on his clothes.

And in that town a dog was found,
As many dogs there be,
Both mongrel, puppy, whelp, and hound,
And curs of low degree.

This dog and man at first were friends;
But when a pique began,
The dog, to gain some private ends,
Went mad and bit the man.

Around from all the neighbouring streets
The wondering neighbours ran,
And swore the dog had lost his wits,
To bite so good a man.

The wound it seem'd both sore and sad
To every Christian eye;
And while they swore the dog was mad,
They swore the man would die.

But soon a wonder came to light,
That show's the rogues they lied:
The man recover'd of the bite,
The dog it was that died.

Jack London

1876-1916

THE CALL OF
THE WILD
Excerpt

When John Thornton froze his feet in the previous December, his partners had made him comfortable and left him to get well, going on themselves up the river to get out a raft of saw logs for Dawson. He was still limping slightly at the time he rescued Buck, but with the continued warm weather even the slight limp left him. And here, lying by the river bank through the long spring days, watching the running water, listening lazily to the songs of birds and the hum of nature, Buck slowly won back his strength.

A rest comes very good after one has traveled three thousand miles, and it must be confessed that Buck waxed lazy as his wounds healed, his muscles swelled out, and the flesh came back to cover his bones. For that matter, they were all loafing—Buck, John Thornton, and Skeet and Nig—waiting for the raft to come that was to carry them down to Dawson. Skeet was a little Irish setter who early made friends with Buck, who, in a dying condition, was unable to resent her first advances. She had the doctor trait which some dogs possess; and as a mother cat washes her kittens so she washed and cleansed Buck's wounds. Regularly, each morning after he had finished his breakfast, she performed her self-appointed task, till he came to look for her ministrations as much as he did for Thornton's. Nig, equally friendly, though less demonstrative, was a huge black dog, half bloodhound and half deerhound, with eyes that laughed and a boundless good nature.

To Buck's surprise these dogs manifested no jealousy toward him. They seemed to share the kindliness and largeness of John Thornton. As Buck grew stronger they enticed him into all sorts of ridiculous games, in which Thornton himself could not forbear to join; and in this fashion Buck romped through his convalescence and into a new existence. Love, genuine passionate love, was his for the first time. This he had never experienced at Judge Miller's down in the sun-kissed Santa Clara Valley. With the Judge's sons, hunting and tramping, it had been a working partnership; with the Judge's grandsons, a sort of pompous guardianship; and with the Judge himself, a stately and dignified friendship. But love that was feverish and burning, that was adoration, that was madness, it had taken John Thornton to arouse.

This man had saved his life, which was something; but, futher, he was the ideal master. Other men saw to the welfare of their dogs from a sense of duty and business expediency; he saw to the welfare of his as if they were his own children, because he could not help it. And he saw further. He never forgot a kindly greeting or a cheering word, and to sit down for a long talk with them (gas, he called it) was as much his delight as theirs. He had a way of taking Buck's head roughly between his hands, and resting his own head upon Buck's, of shaking him back and forth, the while calling him ill names that to Buck were love names. Buck knew no greater joy than that rough embrace and the sound of murmured oaths, and at each jerk back and forth it seemed that his heart would be shaken out of his body so great was its ecstasy. And when, released, he sprang to his feet, his mouth laughing, his eyes eloquent, his throat vibrant with unuttered sound, and in that fashion remained without movement, John Thornton would reverently exclaim, "God! you can all but speak!"

Buck had a trick of love expression that was akin to hurt. He would often seize Thornton's hand in his mouth and close so fiercely that the flesh bore the impress of his teeth for some time afterward. And as Buck understood the oaths to be love words, so the man understood this feigned bite for a caress.

For the most part, however, Buck's love was expressed in adoration. While he went wild with happiness when Thornton touched him or spoke to him, he did not seek these tokens. Unlike Skeet, who was wont to shove her nose under Thornton's hand and nudge and nudge till petted, or Nig, who would stalk up and rest his great head on Thornton's knee, Buck was content to adore at a distance. He would lie by the hour, eager, alert, at Thornton's feet, looking up into his face, dwelling upon it, studying it, following with keenest interest each fleeting expression, every movement or change of feature. Or, as chance might have it, he would lie farther away, to the side or rear, watching the outlines of the man and the occasional movements of his body. And often, such was the communion in which they lived, the strength of Buck's gaze would draw John Thornton's head around, and he would return the gaze, without speech, his heart shining out of his eyes as Buck's heart shone out.

For a long time after his rescue, Buck did not like Thornton to get out of his sight. From the moment he left the tent to when he entered it again, Buck would follow at his heels. His transient masters since he had come into the Northland had bred in him a fear that no master could be permanent. He was afraid that Thornton would pass out of his life as Perrault and François and the Scotch half-breed had passed out. Even in the night, in his dreams, he was haunted by this fear. At such times he would shake off sleep and creep through the chill to the flap of the tent, where he would stand and listen to the sound of his master's breathing.

But in spite of this great love he bore John Thornton, which seemed to bespeak the soft, civilizing influence, the strain of the primitive, which the Northland had aroused in him, remained alive and active. Faithfulness and devotion, things born of fire and roof, were his; yet he retained his wildness and wiliness. He was a thing of the wild, come in from the wild to sit by John Thornton's fire, rather than a dog of the soft Southland stamped with the marks of generations of civilization. Because of his very great love, he could not steal from this man, but from any other man, in any other camp, he did not hesitate an instant; while the cunning with which he stole enabled him to escape detection.

His face and body were scored by the teeth of many dogs, and he fought as fiercely as ever and more shrewdly. Skeet and Nig were too good-natured for quarreling—besides, they belonged to John Thornton; but the strange dog, no matter what the breed or valor, swiftly acknowledged Buck's supremacy or found himself struggling for life with a terrible antagonist. And Buck was merciless. He had learned well the law of club and fang, and he never forwent an advantage or drew back from a foe he had started on the way to Death. He had lessoned from Spitz, and from the chief fighting dogs of the police and mail, and knew there was no middle course. He must master or be mastered; while to show mercy was a weakness. Mercy did not exist in the primordial life. It was misunderstood for fear, and such misunderstandings made for death. Kill or be killed, eat or be eaten, was the law; and this mandate, down out of the depths of Time, he obeyed.

He was older than the days he had seen and the breaths he had drawn. He linked the past with the present, and the eternity behind him throbbed through him in a mighty rhythm to which he swayed as the tides and seasons swayed. He sat by John Thornton's fire, a broad-breasted dog, white-fanged and long-furred; but behind him were the shades of all manner of dogs, half wolves and wild wolves, urgent and prompting, tasting the savor of the meat he ate, thirsting for the water he drank, scenting the wind with him, listening with him and telling him the sounds made by the wild life in the forest, dictating his moods, directing his actions, lying down to sleep with him when he lay down, and dreaming with him and beyond him and becoming themselves the stuff of his dreams.

So peremptorily did these shades beckon him, that each day mankind and the claims of mankind slipped farther from him. Deep in the forest a call

was sounding, and as often as he heard this call, mysteriously thrilling and luring, he felt compelled to turn his back upon the fire and the beaten earth around it, and to plunge into the forest, and on and on, he knew not where or why; nor did he wonder where or why, the call sounding imperiously, deep in the forest. But as often as he gained the soft unbroken earth and the green shade, the love for John Thornton drew him back to the fire again.

Thornton alone held him. The rest of mankind was as nothing. Chance travelers might praise or pet him; but he was cold under it all, and from a too demonstrative man he would get up and walk away. When Thornton's partners, Hans and Pete, arrived on the long-expected raft, Buck refused to notice them till he learned they were close to Thornton; after that he tolerated them in a passive sort of way, accepting favors from them as though he favored them by accepting. They were of the same large type as Thornton, living close to the earth, thinking simply and seeing clearly; and ere they swung the raft into the big eddy by the sawmill at Dawson, they understood Buck and his ways, and did not insist upon an intimacy such as obtained with Skeet and Nig.

For Thornton, however, his love seemed to grow and grow. He, alone among men, could put a pack upon Buck's back in the summer traveling. Nothing was too great for Buck to do, when Thornton commanded. One day (they had grubstaked themselves from the proceeds of the raft and left Dawson for the headwaters of the Tanana) the men and dogs were sitting on the crest of a cliff which fell away, straight down, to naked bedrock three hundred feet below. John Thornton was sitting near the edge, Buck at his shoulder. A thoughtless whim seized Thornton, and he drew the attention of Hans and Pete to the experiment he had in mind. "Jump, Buck!" he commanded, sweeping his arm out and over the chasm. The next instant he was grappling with Buck on the extreme edge, while Hans and Pete were dragging them back into safety.

"It's uncanny," Pete said, after it was over and they had caught their speech.

Thornton shook his head. "No, it is splendid, and it is terrible, too. Do you know, it sometimes makes me afraid."

"I'm not hankering to be the man that lays hands on you while he's around," Pete announced conclusively, nodding his head toward Buck.

"Py Jingo!" was Hans's contribution. "Not mineself either."

It was at Circle City, ere the year was out, that Pete's apprehensions were realized. "Black" Burton, a man evil-tempered and malicious, had been picking a quarrel with a tenderfoot at the bar, when Thornton steeped good-naturedly between. Buck, as was his custom, was lying in a corner, head on paws, watching his master's every action. Burton struck out, without warning, straight from the shoulder. Thornton was sent spinning, and saved himself from falling only by clutching the rail of the bar.

Those who were looking on heard what was neither bark nor yelp, but a something which is best described as a roar, and they saw Buck's body rise up in the air as he left the floor for Burton's throat. The man saved his life by instinctively throwing out his arm, but was hurled backward to the floor with Buck on top of him. Buck loosed his teeth from the flesh of the arm and drove in again for the throat. This time the man succeeded only in partly blocking, and his throat was torn open. Then the crowd was upon Buck, and he was driven off; but while a surgeon checked the bleeding, he prowled up and down, growling furiously, attempting to rush in, and being forced back by an array of hostile clubs. A "miners' meeting," called on the spot, decided that the dog had sufficient provocation, and Buck was discharged. But his reputation was made, and from that day his name spread through every camp in Alaska.

Later on, in the fall of the year, he saved John Thornton's life in quite another fashion. The three partners were lining a long and narrow poling boat down a bad stretch of rapids on the Forty Mile Creek. Hans and Pete moved along the bank, snubbing with a thin Manila rope from tree to tree, while Thornton remained in the boat, helping its descent by means of a pole, and shouting directions to the shore. Buck, on the bank, worried and anxious, kept abreast of the boat, his eyes never off his master.

At a particularly bad spot, where a ledge of barely submerged rocks jutted out into the river, Hans cast off the rope, and, while Thornton poled the boat out into the stream, ran down the bank with the end in his hand to snub the boat when it had cleared the ledge. This it did, and was flying downstream in a current as swift as a millrace, when Hans checked too suddenly. The boat flirted over and snubbed in to the bank bottom up, while Thornton, flung sheer out of it, was carried downstream toward the worst part of the rapids, a stretch of wild water in which no swimmer could live.

Buck had sprung in on the instant; and at the end of three hundred yards, amid a mad swirl of water, he overhauled Thornton. When he felt him grasp his tail, Buck headed for the bank, swimming with all his splendid strength. But the progress shore-ward was slow, the progress downstream amazingly rapid. From below came the fatal roaring where the wild current went wilder and was rent in shreds and spray by the rocks which thrust through like the teeth of an enormous comb. The suck of the water as it took the beginning of the last steep pitch was frightful, and Thornton knew that the shore was impossible. He scraped furiously over a rock, bruised across a second, and struck a third with crushing force. He clutched its slippery top with both hands, releasing Buck, and above the roar of the churning water shouted: "Go, Buck! Go!"

Buck could not hold his own, and swept on downstream, struggling desperately, but unable to win back. When he heard Thornton's command repeated, he partly reared out of the water, throwing his head high, as though for a last look, then turned obediently toward the bank. He swam powerfully and was dragged ashore by Pete and Hans at the very point when swimming ceased to be possible and destruction began.

They knew that the time a man could cling to a slippery rock in the face of that driving current was a matter of minutes, and they ran as fast as they could up the bank to a point far above where Thornton was hanging on. They attached the line with which they had been snubbing the boat to Buck's neck and shoulders, being careful that it should neither strangle him nor impede his swimming, and launched him into the stream. He struck out boldly, but not straight enough into the stream. He discovered the mistake too late, when Thornton was abreast of him and a bare half-dozen strokes away while he was being carried helplessly past.

Hans promptly snubbed with the rope, as though Buck were a boat. The rope thus tightening on him in the sweep of the current, he was jerked under the surface, and under the surface he remained till his body struck against the bank and he was hauled out. He was half drowned, and Hans and Pete threw themselves upon him, pounding the breath into him and the water out of him. He staggered to his feet and fell down. The faint sound of Thornton's voice came to them, and though they could not make out the words of it, they knew that he was in his extremity. His master's voice acted on Buck like an electric shock. He sprang to his feet and ran up the bank ahead of the men to the point of his previous departure.

Again the rope was attached and he was launched, and again he struck out, but this time straight into the stream. He had miscalculated once, but he would not be guilty of it a second time. Hans paid out the rope, permitting no slack, while Pete kept it clear of coils. Buck held on till he was on a line straight

above Thornton; then he turned, and with the speed of an express train headed down upon him. Thornton saw him coming, and, as Buck struck him like a battering ram, with the whole force of the current behind him, he reached up and closed with both arms around the shaggy neck. Hans snubbed the rope around the tree, and Buck and Thornton were jerked under the water. Strangling, suffocating, sometimes one uppermost and sometimes the other, dragging over the jagged bottom, smashing against rocks and snags, they veered in to the bank.

Thornton came to, belly downward and being violently propelled back and forth across a drift log by Hans and Pete. His first glance was for Buck, over whose limp and apparently lifeless body Nig was setting up a howl, while Skeet was licking the wet face and closed eyes. Thornton was himself bruised and battered, and he went carefully over Buck's body, when he had been brought around, finding three broken ribs.

"That settles it," he announced. "We camp right here." And camp they did, till Buck's ribs knitted and he was able to travel.

That winter, at Dawson, Buck performed another exploit, not so heroic, perhaps, but one that put his name many notches higher on the totem pole of Alaskan fame. This exploit was particularly gratifying to the three men; for they stood in need of the outfit which it furnished, and were enabled to make a long-desired trip into the virgin East, where miners had not yet appeared. It was brought about by a conversation in the Eldorado Saloon, in which men waxed boastful of their favorite dogs. Buck, because of his record, was the target for these men, and Thornton was driven stoutly to defend him. At the end of half an hour one man stated that his dog could start a sled with five hundred pounds and walk off with it; a second bragged six hundred for his dog; and a third, seven hundred.

"Pooh! pooh!" said John Thornton; "Buck can start a thousand pounds."

"And break it out! and walk off with it for a hundred yards?" demanded Matthewson, a Bonanza King, he of the seven hundred vaunt.

"And break it out, and walk off with it for hundred yards," John Thornton said coolly.

"Well," Matthewson said, slowly and deliberately, so that all could hear, "I've got a thousand dollars that says he can't. And there it is." So saying, he slammed a sack of gold dust of the size of a bologna sausage down upon the bar.

Nobody spoke. Thornton's bluff, if bluff it was, had been called. He could feel a flush of warm blood creeping up his face. His tongue had tricked him. He did not know whether Buck would start a thousand pounds. Half a ton! The enormousness of it appalled him. He had great faith in Buck's strength and had often thought him capable of starting such a load; but never, as now, had he faced the possibility of it, the eyes of a dozen men fixed upon him, silent and waiting. Further, he had no thousand dollars; nor had Hans or Pete.

"I've got a sled standing outside now, with twenty fifty-pound sacks of flour on it," Matthewson went on with brutal directness; "so don't let that hinder you."

Thornton did not reply. He did not know what to say. He glanced from face to face in the absent way of a man who has lost the power of thought and is seeking somewhere to find the thing that will start it going again. The face of Jim O'Brien, a Mastodon King and old-time comrade, caught his eyes. It was as a cue to him, seeming to rouse him to do what he would never have dreamed of doing.

"Can you lend me a thousand?" he asked, almost in a whisper.

"Sure," answered O'Brien, thumping down a plethoric sack by the side of Matthewson's. "Though it's little faith I'm having, John, that the beast can do the trick."

The Eldorado emptied its occupants into the street to see the test. The tables were deserted, and the dealers and gamekeepers came forth to see the outcome of the wager and to lay odds. Several hundred men, furred and mittened, banked around the sled within easy distance. Matthewson's sled, loaded with a thousand pounds of flour, had been standing for a couple of hours, and in the intense cold (it was sixty below zero) the runners had frozen fast to the hard-packed snow. Men offered odds of two to one that Buck could not budge the sled. A quibble arose concerning the phrase "break out." O'Brien contended it was Thornton's privilege to knock the runners loose, leaving Buck to "break it out" from a dead standstill. Matthewson insisted that the phrase included breaking the runners from the frozen grip of the snow. A majority of the men who had witnessed the making of the bet decided in his favor, whereat the odds went up to three to one against Buck.

There were no takers. Not a man believed him capable of the feat. Thornton had been hurried into the wager, heavy with doubt; and now that he looked at the sled itself, the concrete fact, with the regular team of ten dogs culed up in the snow before it, the more impossible the task appeared. Matthewson waxed jubilant.

"Three to one!" he proclaimed. "I'll lay you another thousand at that figure, Thornton. What d'ye say?"

Thornton's doubt was strong in his face, but his fighting spirit was aroused—the fighting spirit that soars above odds, fails to recognize the impossible, and is deaf to all save the clamor for battle. He called Hans and Pete to him. Their sacks were slim, and with his own, the three partners could rake together only two hundred dollars. In the ebb of their fortunes, this sum was their total capital; yet they laid it unhesitatingly against Matthewson's six hundred.

The team of ten dogs was unhitched, and Buck, with his own harness, was put into the sled. He had caught the contagion of the excitement, and he felt that in some way he must do a great thing for John Thornton. Murmurs of admiration at his splendid appearance went up. He was in perfect condition, without an ounce of superfluous flesh, and the one hundred and fifty pounds that he weighed were so many pounds of grit and virility. His furry coat shone with the sheen of silk. Down the neck and across the shoulders, his mane, in repose as it was, half bristled and seemed to lift with every movement, as though excess of vigor made each particular hair alive and active. The great breast and heavy forelegs were no more than in proportion with the rest of the body, where the muscles showed in tight rolls underneath the skin. Men felt these muscles and proclaimed them hard as iron, and the odds went down to two to one.

"Gad, sir! Gad, sir!" stuttered a member of the latest dynasty, a king of the Skookum Benches. "I offer you eight hundred for him, sir, before the test, sir; eight hundred just as he stands."

Thornton shook his head and stepped to Buck's side.

"You must stand off from him," Matthewson protested. "Free play and plenty of room."

The crowd fell silent; only could be heard the voices of the gamblers vainly offering two to one. Everybody acknowledged Buck a magnificent animal, but twenty fifty-pound sacks of flour bulked too large in their eyes for them to loosen their pouch strings.

Thornton knelt down by Buck's side. He took his head in his two hands and rested cheek to cheek. He did not playfully shake him, as was his wont, or murmur soft love curses; but he whispered in his ear. "As you love me, Buck. As you love me," was what he whispered. Buck whined with suppressed eagerness.

The crowd was watching curiously. The affair was growing mysterious. It seemed like a conjuration. As Thornton got to his feet, Buck seized his mittened hand between his jaws, pressing in with his teeth and releasing slowly, half-reluctantly. It was the answer, in terms, not of speech, but of love. Thornton stepped well back.

"Now, Buck," he said.

Buck tightened the traces, then slacked them for a matter of several inches. It was the way he had learned.

"Gee!" Thornton's voice rang out, sharp in the tense silence.

Buck swung to the right, ending the movement in a plunge that took up the slack and with a sudden jerk arrested his one hundred and fifty pounds. The load quivered, and from under the runners arose a crisp crackling.

"Haw!" Thornton commanded.

Buck duplicated the maneuver, this time to the left. The crackling turned into a snapping, the sled pivoting and the runners slipping and grating several inches to the side. The sled was broken out. Men were holding their breaths, intensely unconscious of the fact.

"Now, MUSH!"

Thornton's command cracked out like a pistol shot. Buck threw himself forward, tightening the traces with a jarring lunge, His whole body was gathered compactly together in the tremendous effort, the muscles writhing and knotting like live things under the silky fur. His great chest was low to the ground, his head forward and down, while his feet were flying like mad, the claws scarring the hard-packed snow in parallel grooves. The sled swayed and trembled, half-started forward. One of his feet slipped, and one man groaned aloud. Then the sled lurched ahead in what appeared a rapid succession of jerks, though it never really came to a dead stop again...half an inch...an inch...two inches....The jerks perceptibly diminished; as the sled gained momentum, he caught them up, till it was moving steadily along.

Men gasped and began to breathe again, unaware for a moment they had ceased to breathe. Thornton was running behind, encouraging Buck with short, cheery words. The distance had been measured off, and as he neared the pile of firewood which marked the end of the hundred yards, a cheer began to grow and grow, which burst into a roar as he passed the firewood and halted at command. Every man was tearing himself loose, even Matthewson. Hats and mittens were flying in the air. Men were shaking hands, it did not matter with whom, and bubbling over in a general incoherent babel.

But Thornton fell on his knees beside Buck. Head was against head, and he was shaking him back and forth. Those who hurried up heard him cursing Buck, and he cursed him long and fervently, and softly and lovingly.

"Gad, sir! Gad, sir!" spluttered the Skookum Bench king. "I'll give you a thousand for him, sir, a thousand, sir—twelve hundred, sir."

Thornton rose to his feet. His eyes were wet. The tears were streaming frankly down his cheeks. "Sir," he said to the Skookum Bench king, "no sir. You can go to hell, sir. It's the best I can do for you, sir."

Buck seized Thornton's hand in his teeth. Thornton shook him back and forth. As though animated by a common impulse, the onlookers drew back to a respectful distance; nor were they again indiscreet enough to interrupt.

History of Quadrupeds

Eighteenth Century

THE DOG

The services of this truly valuable creature have been so eminently useful to the domestic interests of men in all ages, that to give the history of the Dog would be little less than to trace mankind back to their original state of simplicity and freedom, to mark the progress of civilization through the various changes of the world; and to follow attentively the gradual advancement of that order which placed man at the head of the animal world, and gave him a manifest superiority over every part of the brute creation.

If we consider for a moment the state of man without the aid of this useful domestic;—with what arts shall he oppose the numerous hosts of foes that surround him on all sides, seeing every opportunity to encroach upon his possessions, to destroy his labours, or endanger his personal safety? Or how shall he bring into subjection such as are necessary for his well-being? His utmost vigilance will not be sufficient to secure him from the rapacity of the one, nor his greatest exertions enable him to overcome the speed of the other. To maintain his independence, to insure his safety, and to provide for his support, it was necessary that some one among the animals should be brought over to his assistance, whose zeal and fidelity might be depended on: And where, amidst all the various orders of animated being, could one be found so entirely adapted to this purpose? Where could one be found so bold, so tractable, and so obedient, as the Dog?—To confirm the truth of these observations, we need only turn our attention to the present condition of those nations not yet emerged from a state of barbarism, where the uses of the Dog are but little known or attended to, and we will find that they lead a precarious and wretched life of perpetual warfare with the still more savage inhabitants of the forest, with which they are obliged to dispute the possession of their uncultivated fields, and, not unfrequently, to divide with them the fruits of their labours.—From hence we may conclude, that the attention of mankind, in the earliest ages, would be engaged in training and rendering this animal subservient to the important purposes of domestic utility; and the result of this art has been the conquest and peaceable possession of the earth.

Of all animals, the Dog seems most susceptible of change, and most easily modified by difference of climate, food, and education; not only the figure of his body, but his faculties, habits, and dispositions, vary in a surprizing manner: Nothing appears constant in them but their internal conformation, which is alike in all; in every other respect, they are very dissimilar: They vary in size, in figure, in the length of the nose and shape of the head, in the length and direction of the ears and tail, in the colour, quality, and quantity of the hair, &c. To enumerate the different kinds, or mark the discriminations by which each is distinguished, would be a task as fruitless as it would be impossible; to account for this wonderful variety, or investigate the character of the primitive stock from which they have sprung, would be equally vain. Of this only we are certain, that, in every age, Dogs have been found possessed of qualities most admirably adapted for the various purposes to which they have been from time to time applied.—We have seen, in the history of the Cow and the Sheep, that those animals which have been long under the management of man, never preserve the stamp of nature in its original purity. In wild animals, which still enjoy their original freedom from restraint, and have the independent choice of food and climate, this impression is still faithfully preserved; but those which man has subdued, transported from climate to climate, changed their food, habits, and manner of living, must necessarily have suffered the greatest alterations in their form; and as the Dog, of all other domestic animals, is most accustomed to this influence, is endowed with dispositions the most docile and obedient, is susceptible of every impression, and submissive to every restraint, we need not wonder that he should be subject to the greatest variety.—To an attentive observer of the canine race, it is truly wonderful and curious to observe the rapid changes and singular combinations of forms, arising from promiscuous intercourse, which every-where present themselves: They appear in endless succession, and seem more like the effect of whimsical caprice than the regular and uniform production of Nature: So that, in whatever light we consider the various mixtures which at present abound, and render every idea of a systematic arrangement dubious and problematical, we may fairly presume, that the services of the Dog would be first required in maintaining and preserving the superiority of man over those animals which were destined for his support.

All I observed was the silliness of the King playing with his dogs all the while, and not minding the business.
Samuel Pepys

THE DALMATIAN OR COACH DOG

This dog has been erroneously called the *Danish Dog;* and, by M. Buffon, the *Harrier of Bengal;* but for what reason it is difficult to ascertain, as its incapacity of scenting is sufficient to destroy all affinity to any Dog employed in the pursuit of the Hare.

It is very common in this country at present; and is frequently kept in genteel houses, as an elegant attendant on a carriage.—We do not, however, admire the cruel practice of depriving the poor animal of its ears, in order to encrease its beauty: A practice so general, that we do not remember ever to have seen one of these Dogs unmutilated in that way.

THE LARGE WATER-SPANIEL

The drawing of this beautiful animal was made from one of the finest of its kind, in the possession of J. E. Blackett, esq; of Newcastle upon Tyne.

This kind of Dog is valuable for its great docility and attachment to its master. It receives instructions with readiness, and obeys with uncommon alacrity.—Its form is elegant, its hair beautifully curled, its ears long, and its aspect mild and sagacious.—It is fond of the water, and swims well. It is chiefly used in discovering the haunts of wild-ducks and other water fowl; and also in finding birds that have been shot or disabled.

THE FOX-HOUND

No country in Europe can boast of Fox-Hounds equal in swiftness, strength, or agility, to those of Britain; where the utmost attention is paid to their breeding, education, and maintenance. The climate also seems congenial to their nature; for it has been said, that when Hounds of the English breed have been sent into France or other countries, they quickly degenerate, and in some degree lose those qualities for which they were originally so admirable.

In England, the attachment to the chase is in some measure considered as a trait in the national character; consequently, it is not to be wondered at, that our Dogs and Horses should excel all others in that noble diversion. This propensity appears to be encreasing in the nation; and no price seems now thought too great for Hounds of known excellence.

The Fox-Hounds generally preferred are tall, light-made, but strong, and possessed of great courage, speed, and activity.

THE GREYHOUND

M. Buffon supposes the Greyhound to be the Irish Greyhound, rendered thinner and more delicate by the difference of climate and culture: But whatever truth there may be in the fanciful arrangements of that ingenious author, there is an evident familiarity of form; particularly in the depth of the chest, in the length of the legs, and in the smallest of the muzzle.

THE SPRINGER, OR COCKER

The Springer, or Cocker is lively, active, and pleasant; an unwearied pursuer of its game; and very expert in raising woodcocks and snipes from their haunts in woods and marshes, through which it ranges with amazing perseverance.

Of the fame kind is that beautiful little Dog, which, in this country, is well known under the appellation of *King Charles's Dog;* the favourite and constant companion of that monarch, who was generally attended by several of them.—It is still preserved as an idle but innocent companion.—Its long ears, curled hair, and web-feet, evidently point out its alliance with the more useful and active kind last mentioned.

THE BULL-DOG

The Bull-Dog is the fiercest of all the Dog kind, and is probably the most courageous creature in the world. It is low in stature, but very strong and muscular. Its nose is short; and the under jaw projects beyond the upper, which gives it a fierce and unpleasing aspect.—Its courage in attacking the Bull is well known: Its fury in seizing, and its invincible obstinacy in maintaining its hold, are truly astonishing. It always aims at the front; and generally fastens upon the lip, the tongue, the eye, or some part of the face; where it hangs, in spite of every effort of the Bull to disengage himself.

As the Bull-Dog always makes his attack without barking, it is very dangerous to approach him alone, without the greatest precaution.

THE NEWFOUNDLAND DOG

The drawing of this Dog was taken from a very fine one at Eslington, in the county of Northumberland, the seat of Sir H. G. Liddell, bart.—Its dimensions were as follow:—From its nose to the end of its tail, it measured six feet two inches; the length of its tail, one foot ten inches; from one fore foot right over its shoulders to the other, five feet seven inches; girt behind the shoulder, three feet two inches; round its head over its ears, two feet; round the upper part of its fore leg, nine inches and a half. It was web-footed, could swim extremely fast, dive with great ease, and bring up any thing from the bottom of the water. It was naturally fond of fish; and ate raw trouts, or other small fish, out of the nets.

This breed of Dogs was originally brought from the country of which they bear the name, where their great strength and docility render them extremely useful to the settlers on those coasts, who use them in bringing down wood from the interior parts of the country to the seaside.

THE COMFORTER

The Comforter is a most elegant little animal, and is generally kept by the ladies as an attendant of the toilette or the drawing-room.—It is very snappish, ill-natured, and noisy; and does not readily admit the familiarity of strangers.

THE ENGLISH SETTER

The English Setter is a hardy, active, handsome Dog.—Its scent is exquisite; and it ranges with great speed and wonderful perseverance. Its sagacity in discovering the various kinds of game, and its caution in approaching them, are truly astonishing.

THE SHEPHERD'S DOG

This useful animal, ever faithful to his charge, reigns at the head of the flock; where it is better heard, and more attended to, than even the voice of the shepherd. Safety, order, and discipline, are the fruits of his vigilance and activity.

In those large tracts of land which, in many parts of our island, are solely appropriated to the feeding of Sheep and other cattle, this sagacious animal is of the utmost importance. Immense flocks may be seen continually ranging over those extensive wilds, as far as the eye can reach, seemingly without con- troul: Their only guide is the shepherd, attended by his Dog, the constant companion of his toils: It receives his commands, and is always prompt to execute them; it is the watchful guardian of the flock, prevents them from straggling, keeps them together, and conducts them from one part of their pasture to another; it will not suffer any strangers to mix with them, but carefully keeps off every intruder. In driving a number of Sheep to any dis- tant part, a well-trained Dog never fails to confine them to the road, watches every avenue that leads from it; where he takes his stand, threatening every delinquent: He pursues the stragglers, if any should escape; and forces them into order, without doing them the least injury.

THE MASTIFF

The Mastiff is much larger and stronger than the Bull-Dog; its ears are more pendulous; its lips are large and loose; its affect is sullen and grave, and its bark loud and terrific.—He seems every way formed for the important trust of guarding and securing the valuable property committed to his care. Houses, gardens, yards, &c. are safe from de- predations whilst in his custody. Confined during the day, as soon as the gates are locked, he is left to range at full liberty: He then goes round the premises, examines every part of them, and by loud barkings gives notice that he is ready to defend his charge.

Dr. Caius, in his curious treatise on British Dogs, tells us, that three of their animals were reckoned a match for a Bear, and four for a Lion.

THE TERRIER

The Terrier has a most acute smell, is generally an attendant on every pack of Hounds, and is very expert in forcing Foxes or other game out of their coverts. It is the determined enemy of all the ver- min kind; such as Weasels, Foumarts, Badgers, Rats, Mice, &c. It is fierce, keen, and hardy; and, in its encounters with the Badger, sometimes meets with very severe treatment, which it sustains with great courage and fortitude: A well-trained veteran Dog frequently proves more than a match for that hard-bitten animal.

27

Lewis Carroll

1832-1898

A VISIT
TO DOG LAND

There's a house, away there to the left', said Sylvie after we had walked what seemed to me about fifty miles. 'Let's go and ask for a night's lodging'.

'It looks a very comfable house', Bruno said, as we turned into the road leading up to it. 'I doos hope the Dogs will be kind to us, I *is* so tired and hungry!'

A Mastiff, dressed in a scarlet collar, and carrying a musket, was pacing up and down, like a sentinel, in front of the entrance. He started, on catching sight of the children, and came forwards to meet them, keeping his musket pointed straight at Bruno, who stood quite still, though he turned pale and kept tight hold of Sylvie's hand, while the Sentinel walked solemnly round and round them, and looked at them from all points of view.

'Oobooh, hooh boohooyah!' he growled at last. 'Woobah yahwah oobooh! Bow wahbah woobooyah? Bow wow?' he asked Bruno, severely.

Of course *Bruno* understood all this, easily enough. All Fairies understand Doggee—that is, Dog-language. But, as *you* may find it a little difficult, just at first, I had better put it into English for you. 'Humans, I verily believe! A couple of stray Humans! What Dog do you belong to? What do you want?'

'We don't belong to a *Dog*!' Bruno began, in Doggee. ('People *never* belongs to Dogs!' he whispered to Sylvie.)

But Sylvie hastily checked him, for fear of hurting the Mastiff's feelings. 'Please, we want a little food, and a night's lodging—if there's room in the house', she added timidly. Sylvie spoke Doggee very prettily: but I think it's almost better, for *you*, to give the conversation in English.

'The *house*, indeed!' growled the Sentinel. 'Have you never seen a *Palace* in your life? Come along with me! His Majesty must settle what's to be done with you'.

They followed him through the entrance-hall, down a long passage, and into a magnificent Saloon, around which were grouped dogs of all sorts and sizes. Two splendid Blood-hounds were solemnly sitting up, one on each side of the crown-bearer. Two or three Bull-dogs—whom I guessed to be the Body-Guard of the King—were waiting in grim silence: in fact the only voices at all plainly audible were those of two little dogs, who had mounted a settee, and were holding a lively discussion that looked very like a quarrel.

'Lords and Ladies in Waiting, and various Court Officials', our guide gruffly remarked, as he led us in. Of *me* the Courtiers took no notice whatever: but Sylvie and Bruno were the subject of many inquisitive looks, and many whispered remarks, of which I only distinctly caught *one*—made by a sly-looking Dachshund to his friend—'Bah wooh wahyah hoobah Oobooh, *hah* bah?' ('She's not such a bad-looking Human, *is* she?')

Leaving the new arrivals in the centre of the Saloon, the Sentinel advanced to a door, at the further end of it, which bore an inscription, painted on it in Doggee, 'Royal Kennel—Scratch and Yell'.

Before doing this, the Sentinel turned to the children, and said 'Give me your names'.

'We'd rather not!' Bruno exclaimed, pulling Sylvie away from the door. 'We want them ourselves. Come back, Sylvie! Come quick!'

'Nonsense!' said Sylvie very decidedly: and gave their names in Doggee.

Then the Sentinel scratched violently at the door, and gave a yell that made Bruno shiver from head to food.

'Hooyah wah!' said a deep voice inside. (That's Doggee for 'Come in!')

'It's the King himself!' the Mastiff whispered in an awestruck tone. 'Take off your wigs, and lay them humbly at his paws'. (What *we* should call 'at his *feet*'.)

Sylvie was just going to explain, very politely, that they *couldn't* perform *that* ceremony, because their wigs wouldn't come off, when the door of the Royal Kennel opened, and an enormous Newfoundland Dog put his head out. 'Bow wow?' was his first question.

When His Majesty speaks to you', the Sentinel hastily whispered to Bruno, 'you should prick up your ears!'

Bruno looked doubtfully at Sylvie. 'I'd rather not, please', he said. 'It would hurt'.

'It doesn't hurt a bit!' the Sentinel said with some indignation. 'Look! It's like this!' And he pricked up his ears like two railway signals.

Sylvie gently explained matters. 'I'm afraid we can't manage it', she said in a low voice. 'I'm very sorry: but our ears haven't got the right———' she wanted to say 'machinery' in Doggee: but she had forgotten the word, and could only think of 'steam-engine'.

The Sentinel repeated Sylvie's explanation to the King.

'Can't prick up their ears without a steam-engine!' His Majesty exclaimed. 'They *must* be curious creatures! I must have a look at them!' And he came out of his Kennel, and walked solemnly up to the children.

What was the amazement—not to say the horror —of the whole assembly, when Sylvie actually *patted His Majesty on the head*, while Bruno seized his long ears and pretended to tie them together under his chin!

The Sentinel groaned aloud: a beautiful Greyhound—who appeared to be one of the Ladies in Waiting—fainted away: and all the other Courtiers hastily drew back, and left plenty of room for the hugh Newfoundland to spring upon the audacious strangers, and tear them limb from limb.

Only—he didn't. On the contrary His Majesty actually *smiled*—so far as a Dog *can* smile—and (the other Dogs couldn't believe their eyes, but it was true, all the same) His Majesty *wagged his tail!*

'Yah! Hooh hahwooh!' (that is 'Well! I never!') was the universal cry.

His Majesty looked round him severely, and gave a slight growl, which produced instant silence. 'Conduct *my friends* to the banqueting-hall!' he said, laying such emphasis on *"my friends"* that several of the dogs rolled over helplessly on their backs and began to lick Bruno's feet.

A procession was formed, but I only ventured to follow as far as the *door* of the banqueting-hall, so furious was the uproar of barking dogs within. So I sat down by the King, who seemed to have gone to sleep, and waited till the children returned to say good-night, when His Majesty got up and shook himself.

'Time for bed!' he said with a sleepy yawn. 'The attendants will show you your room', he added, aside, to Sylvie and Bruno. 'Bring lights!' And, with a dignified air, he held out his paw for them to kiss.

But the children were evidently not well practised in Court-manners. Sylvie simply stroked the

great paw: Bruno hugged it: the Master of Ceremonies looked shocked.

All this time Dog-waiters, in splendid livery, were running up with lighted candles: but, as fast as they put them upon the table, other waiters ran away with them.

The next thing I remember is that it was morning: breakfast was just over: Sylvie was lifting Bruno down from a high chair, and saying to a Spaniel, who was regarding them with a most benevolent smile, 'Yes, thank you, we've had a *very* nice breakfast. Haven't we, Bruno?'

'There was too many bones in the———' Bruno began, but Sylvie frowned at him, and laid her finger to her lips, for, at this moment, the travelers were waited on by a very dignified officer, the Head-Growler, whose duty it was, first to conduct them to the King to bid him farewell, and then to escort them to the boundary of Dogland. The great Newfoundland received them most affably, but, instead of saying 'good-bye,' he startled the Head-Growler into giving three savage growls, by announcing that he would escort them himself.

'It is a most unusual proceeding, your Majesty!' the Head-Growler exclaimed, almost choking with vexation at being set aside, for he had put on his best Court-suit, made entirely of cat-skins, for the occasion.

'I shall escort them myself,' His Majesty repeated, gently but firmly, laying aside the Royal robes, and changing his crown for a small coronet, 'and you may stay at home.'

'I *are* glad!' Bruno whispered to Sylvie, when they had got well out of hearing. 'He were so *welly* cross!' And he not only patted their Royal escort, but even hugged him round the neck in the exuberance of his delight.

His Majesty calmly wagged the Royal tail. 'It's quite a relief,' he said, 'getting away from the Palace now and then! Royal Dogs have a dull life of it, I can tell you! Would you mind' (this to Sylvie, in a low voice, and looking a little shy and embarrassed) 'would you mind the trouble of just throwing that stick for me to fetch?'

Sylvie was too much astonished to do anything for a moment: it sounded such a monstrous impossibility that a *King* should wish to run after a stick. But *Bruno* was equal to the occasion, and with a glad shout of 'Hi then! Fetch it, good Doggie!' he hurled it over a clump of bushes. The next moment the Monarch of Dogland had bounded over the bushes, and picked up the stick, and came galloping back to the children with it in his mouth. Bruno took it from him with great decision. 'Beg for it!' he insisted; and His Majesty begged. 'Paw!' com-

manded Sylvie; and His Majesty gave his paw. In short, the solemn ceremony of escorting the travelers to the boundaries of Dogland became one long uproarious game of play!

'But business is business!' the Dog-King said at last. 'And I must go back to mine. I couldn't come any further,' he added, consulting a dog-watch, which hung on a chain round his neck, 'not even if there were a *Cat* in sight!'

They took an affectionate farewell of His Majesty, and trudged on.

Henry Mayhew

1812-1887

THE DOG
STEALERS

These dog appropriators, as they found that they could levy contributions not only on royalty, foreign ambassadors, peers, courtiers, and ladies of rank, but on public bodies, and on the dignitaries of the state, the law, the army, and the church, became bolder and more expert in their avocations—a boldness which was encouraged by the existing law. The only mode of punishment for dog-stealing was by summary conviction, the penalty being fine or imprisonment; but Mr. Commissioner Mayne did not know of any instance of a dog-stealer being sent to prison in default of payment. Although the law recognised no property in a dog, the animals was taxed; and it was complained at the time that an unhappy lady might have to pay tax for the full term upon her dog, perhaps a year and a half after he had been stolen from her. One old offender, who stole the Duke of Beaufort's dog, was transported, not for stealing the dog, but his collar.

The difficulty of proving the positive theft of a dog was extreme. In most cases, where the man was not seen actually to seize the dog which could be identified, he escaped when carried before a magistrate. 'The dog-stealers,' said Inspector Shackell, 'generally go two together; they have a piece of liver, they say it is merely bullock's liver, which will entice or tame the wildest or savagest dog which there can be in any yard; they give it to him, and take him from his chain. At other times, they will go in the street with a little dog, rubbed over with some sort of stuff, and will entice valuable dogs away…If there is a dog lost or stolen, it is generally known within five or six hours where that dog is, and they know almost exactly what they can get for it, so that it is a regular system of plunder.' Mr. G. White, 'dealer in live stock, dogs, and other

animals', and at one time 'dealer in lions, and tigers, and all sorts of things', said of the dog-stealers; 'In turning the corners of streets there are two or three of them together; one will snatch up a dog and put it into his apron, and the others will stop the lady and say, "What is the matter?" and direct the party who has lost the dog in a contrary direction to that taken'.

In this business were engaged from 50 to 60 men, half of them actual stealers of the animals. The others were the receivers, and the go-betweens or 'restorers'. The thief kept the dog perhaps for a day or two at some public-house, and he then took it to a dog-dealer with whom he was connected in the way of business. These dealers carried on a trade in 'honest dogs', but some of them dealt principally with the dog-stealers. Their depots could not be entered by the police, being private premises, without a search-warrant—and direct evidence was necessary to obtain a search-warrant—and of course a stranger in quest of a stolen dog would not be admitted. Some of the dog-dealers would not purchase or receive dogs known to have been stolen, but others bought and speculated in them. If an advertisement appeared offering a reward for the dog, a negotiation was entered into. If no reward was offered, the owner of the dog, who was always either known or made out, was waited upon by a restorer, who undertook 'to restore the dog if terms could be come to'. If the person robbed paid a good round sum for the restoration of a dog, and paid it speedily, the animal was almost certain to be stolen a second time, and a higher sum was then demanded. Sometimes the thieves threatened that if they were any longer trifled with they would inflict torture on the dog, or cut its throat. One lady, Miss Brown of Bolton-street, was so worried by these threats, and by having twice to redeem her dog, 'that she has left England', said Mr. Bishop, 'and I really do believe for the sake of keeping the dog'.

Elizabeth Barrett Browning
1806-1861

FLUSH

Well; but Flushie! It is too true that he has been lost—lost and won; and true besides that I was a good deal upset by it *meo more*; and that I found it hard to eat and sleep as usual while he was in the hands of his enemies. It is a secret too. We would not tell papa of it. Papa would have been angry with the unfortunate person who took Flush out without a chain; and would have kicked against the pricks of the necessary bribing of the thief in order to the getting him back. Therefore we didn't tell papa; and as I had a very bad convenient headache the day my eyes were reddened, I did not see him (except once) till Flush was on the sofa again. As to the thieves, you are very kind to talk daggers at them; and I feel no inclination to say 'Don't'. It is quite too bad and cruel. And think of their exceeding insolence in taking Flush away from this very door, while Arabel was waiting to have the door opened on her return from her walk; and in observing (as they gave him back for six guineas and a half) that they intended to have him again at the earliest opportunity and that *then* they must have ten guineas! I tell poor Flushie (while he looks very earnestly in my face) that he and I shall be ruined at last, and that I shall have no money to buy him cakes; but the worst is the anxiety! Whether I am particularly silly, or not, I don't know; they say here, that I am; but it seems to me impossible for anybody who really cares for a dog, to think quietly of his being in the hands of those infamous men. And then I know poor Flushie must feel it. When he was brought home he began to cry in his manner, whine, as if his heart was full! It was just what I was inclined to do myself—'and thus was Flushie lost and won'.

MR. JINGLE'S "PONTO"

Ah! you should keep dogs—fine animals—sagacious creatures—dog of my own once—Pointer—surprising instinct—out shooting one day—entering inclosure—whistled—dog stopped—whistled again—Ponto—no go: stock still—called him—Ponto, Ponto—wouldn't move—dog transfixed—staring at a board—looked up, saw an inscription—'Gamekeeper has orders to shoot all dogs found in this inclosure'—wouldn't pass it—wonderful dog—valuable dog that—very.

The Pickwick Papers,
Charles Dickens

COPPERFIELD MEETS "JIP"

I approached him tenderly, for I loved even him; but he showed his whole set of teeth, got under a chair expressly to snarl, and wouldn't hear of the least familiarity.

David Copperfield,
Charles Dickens

Edward Lear

1812-1888

LIMERICKS

There was an Old Man of Ancona,
Who found a small Dog with no Owner,
    Which he took up and down
    All the streets of the town;
That anxious Old Man of Ancona.

There was a Young Lady of Corsica,
Who purchased a little brown Saucy-cur;
    Which she fed upon Ham
    And hot Raspberry Jam,
That expensive Young Lady of Corsica.

There was a Young Lady of Ryde,
Whose shoe-strings were seldom untied.
    She purchased some clogs,
    And some small spotted dogs,
And frequently walked about Ryde.

There was an Old Man of Leghorn,
The smallest that ever was born;
    But quickly snapped up he
    Was once by a puppy,
Who devoured that Old Man of Leghorn.

There was an Old Man of Kamschatka,
Who possessed a remarkably fat cur;
    His gait and his waddle
    Were held as a model
To all the fat dogs in Kamschatka.

How odd that people of sense should find any pleasure in being accompanied by a beast who is always spoiling conversation. *Lord Macaulay*

OUR DACHSHUND

There lived with us a wagging humorist
In that hound's arch dwarf-legged on boxing-gloves.
George Meredith

THE DACHSHUND

We stroke thy broad, brown paws again,
We bid thee to thy vacant chair,
We greet thee by the window-pane,
We hear thy scuffle on the stair;
We see the flaps of thy large ears
Quick raised to ask which way to go.

Matthew Arnold | 33

Old Mother Hubbard
Went to the cupboard
   To get her poor dog a bone;
But when she came there
The cupboard was bare,
   And so the poor dog had none.

LESSON 14.

See my dog.
See my dog Jep.
See my dog Jep run.

LESSON 26.

The boy sat on a log.
The dog got his hat, and off he ran.

Now let the boy get his hat if he can.

LESSON 54.

I saw the man go by.
He had a bad dog.
If I see a bad dog, I say, "Get out, you cur!"
A bad dog is a *cur*.

LESSON 61.

I see he is an old dog. He can not run far', can he'?

No; he is too old to run far now: but he can dig. He can dig up the sod.
Pet! go and dig.
Do you see him'?
You see he *can* dig.

He dug up an old tin cup one day.

LESSON 62.

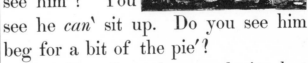

Do you see the hen and the bug'?
Do you see the dog and the fox'?
Let the hen run for the bug, and let her get the bug if she can.

LESSON 67.

Bob', see my dog Jep`. He is not a *big* dog, but he is a *gay* one.

He is fat, too. See his fat leg'!

Now, Jep, sit up if you can. Do as I bid you. Let us all see if you can sit up.

Now do you see him'? You see he *can`* sit up. Do you see him beg for a bit of the pie'?

Yes, Ben, I see he can do it; but my *big* dog can do it too.

I can pat my dog. Can you pat Jep'? Can you pat his paw'? Can you pat him on his ear'?

O, how my dog can run`! He can run to the lot, and get the cow.

Exercise for Lesson 67. Change to question, with *Why?*

Jep is not the big dog.
The big dog was not so gay as Jep.
The big dog did not eat the pie.

Jep did not get the cow.

Gerald Carson

1899-

THE MOST
CELEBRATED
DOG CASE
EVER TRIED IN
JOHNSON COUNTY,
MISSOURI —
OR THE WORLD

It is generally agreed that the dog was the first animal to be domesticated by man, probably because of the clear advantages of a mutual-assistance pact based upon cooperation in the search for food. The dog had the nose. The man had the eyes. The dog was faster, the man more cunning. At any rate, social relations developed between these two, and man found that he could not, or at least would not, get along without the dog. The Egyptians named the brightest star in the heavens the dog star, Sirius. Well-placed Romans kept a dog in the atrium and set in the walls of their dwellings a mosaic or drawing calling attention to the watchdog's fidelity in the words of *cave canem*—"beware of the dog." A legal doctrine even developed in English jurisprudence to the effect that a dog's character was presumed to be good until the contrary was shown. But the greatest literary tribute extant to the qualities of man's ancient companion waited upon a court drama that was played out in a small, dingy courtroom in the west central Missouri. The year was 1869, a time when the average rural American believed implicitly in his watch, the patent medicine of his choice, and his own, personal dog. The central figure in the Missouri case was "Old Drum," a black-and-tan foxhound, with perhaps a little bloodhound in him, who was executed as a supposed killer of sheep, five miles southwest of the hamlet of Kingsville in Johnson County—near the Cass County line. Old Drum found his agony and apotheosis on a still October night and lives on today as part of our national memory and in Missouri's dusty legal reports disguised as *Charles Burden, Respondent* v. *Leonidas Hornsby, Appellant.*

Game was still abundant in the post-Civil War years along the heavily timbered ridges of Johnson County, and Charles Burden, farmer, woodsman, and hunter—a character right out of James Fenimore Cooper—kept a pack of hounds for the chase. Old Drum was the leader and favorite, *primus inter pares*—"first among equals." Some dogs would follow false trails. But not Drum. Burden knew from his bugling music, sounding from the woodlots or tangled undergrowth, what kind of game Old Drum had flushed. In the vernacular of the hunter, the dog "never lied."

"He was good for varmints, wolves, and such like," Burden said, "and was as good a deer dog as I ever had.... Money wouldn't have bought him."

If you are familiar with the habits of the Missouri hound dog, you know that he lies around the place all day, sunning himself, snapping at flies, languidly scratching, apparently no good to himself or anyone else—a real hard-core welfare type. But about dusk he gets restless, yawns, stretches, and soon is ready to hit the trail. On the morning of October 28, Charles Burden, at peace with himself and the world, rode through the glories of the Missouri autumn past the house of his brother-in-law, "Lon" Hornsby, who raised sheep and cattle about a mile north of his own farm; and on to the post office and general store at Kingsville. He returned by the same road to be greeted as usual by Old Drum who leaped upon him, licking his hands and wagging an eager welcome. These were all little details that Burden recalled later. For that night Old Drum met his death and became the subject of legal battles that occupied the attention of four courts before the controversy ended.

It was after sundown. Burden and a neighbor were sitting in the dusk at the front of the house, smoking some of Burden's home-grown tobacco, listening to the baying of pack. Joyous melody announced to their practiced ears that a fox was up and running across the open prairies, along a wooded creek, and into the hills; Old Drum was in the lead, as usual. Suddenly, at about eight o'clock, Burden heard a gun-shot. It came from the direction of Hornsby's farm. There was silence. Then the dogs were baying again. But Old Drum's voice was missing. Burden jumped to his feet, ran to get his hunting horn, and blew several blasts. All the dogs returned except one. Old Drum was not among them.

The next morning Burden saddled up and called on Lon Hornsby, a small, wiry man with flaming red hair and a quarrelsome disposition. During the summer and fall Hornsby had lost a number of sheep, killed by marauding dogs that had also raided his smokehouse. Hornsby had sworn that he would kill the first strange dog he found on his premises. He was making cider when Burden rode up.

"Lon, have you seen anything of my dog Drum around here?" When Hornsby said no, Burden persisted. "What dog was that you shot last night?" Hornsby acknowledged that he did have Dick Ferguson, his young nephew, shoot at a stray dog, "a black-looking dog," but the gun was only loaded with grains of corn, just to scare the rascal. Besides, everybody knew that Drum was not black, but had a black-and-tan coat.

Nevertheless, Old Drum was dead. Burden found

him just above the ford on Big Creek below Hay-maker's mill—about a mile from Hornsby's farm—laying with his head in the water. His body was filled with buckshot. There was mud on his underside, and there were sorrel hairs on the body, indicating that he had been transported and dragged some distance. Hornsby owned a sorrel mule. The evidence was circumstantial, but Burden brought suit for damages before a justice of the peace at Kingsville. One jury failed to come to an agreement, but in a second trial Burden won the verdict. A curious historical footnote to the trial is that one of Hornsby's attorneys was David Nation, later the husband of the muscular temperance fanatic and mystic Carrie Nation, who wielded her little hatchet so destructively in the hotel bars and saloons of Kansas.

Hornsby appealed to the Johnson County Court of Common Pleas at Warrensburg where in March, 1870, the earlier decision was upset. With Hornsby now ahead, it was neighbor against neighbor throughout the community. Threats were made on both sides. One Hornsby witness was warned he would be horsewhipped if he persisted in his testimony, and he prudently disappeared. Refusing to give up, Burden hired the Sedalia, Missouri, law firm of John F. Phillips and George Graham Vest, then the leading lawyers in that part of the state. The former later became a federal judge, the latter, a United States senator.

A new trial was obtained on the ground of new evidence. Once again the whole countryside gathered for court day in the old courthouse on North Main Street in Warrensburg. Everybody was on tenterhooks to know what a jury of farmers and fox hunters would do about convicting or exonerating Old Drum. Hornsby was also represented by able counsel, Thomas T. Crittenden, who later became governor of the state and broke up the Jesse James gang of outlaws, and Francis Marion Cockrell, who later served along with his adversary, Vest, in the United States Senate. Together, these men were known as the "Big Four" of the Missouri bar.

The most colorful figure in the courtroom was Vest, the Kentucky-born descendant of Scotch-Irish Presbyterians from Virginia. He was a graduate of Centre College in Danville, Kentucky, and had read law in the office of James Harlan, lawyer, legislator, and attorney general of Kentucky, and father of John Marshall Harlan, who became an associate justice of the U.S. Supreme Court. In 1852, Vest

graduated from the law department of Transylvania University. He settled in Missouri in 1859, entered into political affairs and was a Democratic Presidential elector on the Douglas ticket. When the Civil War came, Vest enlisted in the Confederate Army and, toward the end of the war, sat in the Senate of the Confederate States. A few years after the Old Drum case, Vest was elected to the U.S. Senate, thus acquiring the distinction of having sat in the highest legislative body of two nations.

At the time of the litigation over Old Drum, Vest was forty years old, one of the coming men of the state, an accomplished stump speaker—witty and emotional by turns—at his best in pleading before a jury, where he demonstrated a mastery of the forensic style then greatly admired. The trial was held on a rainy night in the dim light of kerosine lamps. Many witnesses were heard, including Hornsby's nephew, Dick Ferguson, who ingenuously declared on the witness stand, "My stars! I haven't seen Old Drum since I shot him." During this trial, according to the *Kansas City Star*, in a retelling of the story, "more oratory was turned loose than was ever heard in the most celebrated murder case ever tried in a Missouri court."

All of the arguments have long been forgotten, except Vest's closing appeal. A man of medium height and slender build, with a large head, drooping mustache, magnetic eyes, and great charm of manner, Vest had up to this time taken only a minor part in the proceedings. But now it fell to him to sum up the case against Hornsby. Gravely addressing the presiding judge in the traditional words, "May it please the Court," Vest began to speak quietly and earnestly. He ignored the testimony. For about an hour he ranged through history, poetry, legend, and classical literature calling attention to sagacious and faithful dogs whom men have loved, quoting from the Biblical account of the dogs who came to lick the sores of the beggar Lazarus; citing Byron's line in Don Juan, "'Tis sweet to hear the honest watchdog's bark'"; and the graphic description in John Lothrop Motley's *The Rise of the Dutch Republic* of how a dog had prevented the capture of William of Orange by the cruel Duke of Alva.

After pointing out the weaknesses in the arguments of opposing counsel and drawing attention to the law applicable to the case, Vest appeared ready to conclude. But then he moved closer to the jury box. He looked—someone remembered afterward—taller than his five feet six inches, and began in a quiet voice to deliver an extemporaneous peroration. It was quite brief, less than four hundred words.

"Gentlemen of the jury," Vest said, "the best friend

a man has in the world may turn against him and become his worst enemy. His son or daughter that he has reared with loving care may prove ungrateful. Those who are nearest and dearest to us, those whom we trust with our happiness and our good name, may become traitors to their faith. The money that a man has, he may lose. It flies away from him, perhaps when he needs it the most. A man's reputation may be sacrificed in a moment of ill-considered action. The people who are prone to fall on their knees to do us honor when success is with us may be the first to throw the stone of malice when failure settles its cloud upon our heads. The one absolutely unselfish friend that a man can have in this selfish world, the one that never deserts him and the one that never proves ungrateful or treacherous is his dog.

"Gentlemen of the jury," Vest said, "the best friend him in prosperity and in poverty, in health and in sickness. He will sleep on the cold ground, where the wintry winds blow and the snow drives fiercely, if only he may be near his master's side. He will kiss the hand that has no food to offer, he will lick the wounds and sores that come in encounters with the roughness of the world. He guards the sleep of his pauper master as if he were a prince. When all other friends desert he remains. When riches take wings and reputation falls to pieces, he is as constant in his love as the sun in its journey through the heavens. If fortune drives the master forth an outcast in the world, friendless and homeless, the faithful dog asks no higher privelege than that of accompanying him to guard against danger, to fight against his enemies, and when the last scene of all comes, and death takes the master in its embrace and his body is laid away in the cold ground, no matter if all other friends pursue their way, there by his graveside will the noble dog be found, his head between his paws, his eyes sad but open in alert watchfulness, faithful and true even to death."

When Vest had concluded, he bowed to the judge and sat down. The presiding justice was entranced. Great sobs shook the courtroom. Hounds of the Old Drum type were "folks," a part of the family, on the middle border a hundred years ago. For a magic moment the spectators were transported, uplifted by the loneliness and ultimate tragedy of all life that struck home to all who heard the appeal. Seeing themselves as in a mirror, the jury wept.

Crittenden, one of the adverse attorneys, leaned over to his associate Cockrell, and whispered, as he recalled later that the dog, though dead, had won. He added, "we had better get out of the courthouse with our client, or all would be hanged," Vest's closing words, in which he depicted the "noble dog" at

his master's grave, was not sheer hyperbole. Such a dog actually existed at the time in Scotland. His name was "Greyfriars Bobby" and he guarded the grave of his owner from 1858 to his own death in 1872. As Greyfriars Bobby's fame spread, the Lord Provost exempted him from the dog tax and a fountain was raised in his honor at Edinburgh by Angela, Baroness Burdett-Coutts, noted philanthropist and close friend of Queen Victoria. Another instance of the faithfullness of dog to man comes from nearer home. Lucien B. Kerr, Colonel of the Eleventh Illinois Cavalry, survived the Civil War but was fatally wounded in a hunting accident. The Irish setter that had accompanied him was inconsolable. While the Colonel lay near death at his home in Peoria, the dog, according to one account, stationed himself on the veranda outside the sick room. When Kerr refused amputation of his arm and died, the dog was allowed to enter the room. He put his paws on the bed, licked the face of his dead master, returned to his post on the porch, and died within the hour. Perhaps, from the perspective of a more skeptical age, this may be regarded as an instance of the pathetic fallacy. Perhaps the dog had the distemper. But it is a fact that on the northwest corner of Colonel Kerr's lot in Peoria's Springdale Cemetery, there is a reclining dog "true, even unto death," sculptured in sandstone.

The Old Drum jury took two minutes to return a verdict in favor of Burden and assess damages of $50. For his tribute to all dogdom, Vest received a fee of $10. Hornsby appealed to the Missouri Supreme Court, but his heart was not really in it, and when the decision of the lower court was affirmed, the case ground to an end. Old Drum had been vindicated and given a martyr's crown in what one law journal called "the most celebrated dog case in Johnson County, Missouri, or for that matter, in the world."

No court stenographer was present when Senator Vest pronounced his eulogy, and his words are sometimes referred to as the "Lost Speech." But it has been carefully reconstructed from notes taken by Crittenden and has survived, not because it was written or printed but, as Professor William Lyon Phelps once pointed out, "in the same manner as ancient epics, folk songs, ballads, cowboy choruses, sea chanteys, and lullabies." Vest's gem of sentiment on an aspect of the human—animal relationship has completely overshadowed his long and important career in the United States Senate from 1879 to 1903, a period when he had, according to the *Chicago Journal*, "half the brains of the Democratic side of the Senate." Vest opposed the high protective measures of his day, the acquisition of territory after the

Spanish-American War, and on one occasion, thwarted an attempt by private interests to commercialize Yellowstone Park.

The eulogy was quickly recognized as a classic statement and has never disappeared from view since it was delivered. Some two years after Senator Vest's death in 1904, the speech was revived as a funeral oration over the grave of a dog, Pero, killed by an automobile in Denver. It became almost axiomatic for any attorney representing the owner of a slain animal to talk about men and dogs and what they mean to each other, invoking, of course, the memory of Old Drum. But courtroom procedures have changed with the passing years, and Old Drum may be near the end of his century of service so far as the higher courts are concerned. The Missouri Supreme Court recently set aside the conviction of a man who had killed another man's dog. The ruling was made on the ground that the lawyer for the dog's owner had improperly injected Old Drum into the case for its emotional effect upon the jury.

Regardless of what the courts may say about the legal proprieties, Old Drum has not lost his hold on the affections of dog owners. A bronze tablet has been attached to the wall of the old court house in Warrensburg, now the home of the Johnson County Historical Society, marking the scene as a historic site. Another monument stands on the banks of Big Creek just above the deer crossing where Drum was found after he was shot. The memorial includes in its construction rocks sent from most of the American states, the Great Wall of China, the white cliffs of Dover, Germany, France, Guatemala, Mexico, Jamaica, South Africa, the Virgin Islands, Panama, and the West Indies. The base bears a granite stone on which is incised the representation of a dog treeing a coon. A deer is being chased in one corner, a fox in the other. The lettering reads "Old Drum—Killed 1869." A bronze statue, executed by Reno Gastaldi, the St. Louis sculptor, stands on the lawn of the present court house, the model created from a study of some of the best hound dogs in the Middle West. It was dedicated in 1953 by the attorney general of Missouri and Captain Will Judy of Chicago, editor of *Dog World*. The text of the Old Drum speech appears on the marble base.

Burden and Hornsby eventually recovered from the economic effects of their litigation, were reconciled, and died in obscurity. But the dog they fought over seems destined to be remembered as long as men shall enjoy the companionship of a canine friend.

When a dog bites a man that is not news, but when a man bites a dog that is news. *Charles A. Dana*

W. H. Hudson
1841-1922

DANDY

He was of mixed breed, and was supposed to have a strain of Dandy Dinmont blood which gave him his name. A big ungainly animal with a rough shaggy coat of blue-gray hair and white on his neck and clumsy paws. He looked like a Sussex sheep dog with legs reduced to half their proper length. He was, when I first knew him, getting old and increasingly deaf and dim of sight, otherwise in the best of health and spirits, or at all events very good-tempered.

Until I knew Dandy I had always supposed that the story of Ludlam's dog was pure invention, and I dare say that is the general opinion about it; but Dandy made me reconsider the subject, and eventually I came to believe that Ludlam's dog did exist once upon a time, centuries ago perhaps, and that if he had been the laziest dog in the world Dandy was not far behind him in that respect. It is true he did not lean his head against a wall to bark; he exhibited his laziness in other ways. He barked often, though never at strangers; he welcomed every visitor, even the tax-collector, with tail-waggings and a smile. He spent a good deal of his time in the large kitchen, where he had a sofa to sleep on, and when the two cats of the house wanted an hour's rest they would coil themselves up on Dandy's broad shaggy side, preferring that bed to cushion or rug. They were like a warm blanket over him, and it was a sort of mutual benefit society. After an hour's sleep Dandy would go out for a short constitutional as far as the neighboring thoroughfare, where he would blunder against people, wag his tail to everybody, and then come back. He had six or eight or more outings each day, and, owing to doors and gates being closed and to his lazy disposition, he had much trouble in getting out and in. First he would sit down in the hall and bark, bark, bark, until some one would come to open the door for him, whereupon he would slowly waddle down the garden path, and if he found the gate closed he would again sit down and start barking. And the bark, bark would go on until some one came to let him out. But if after he had barked about twenty or thirty times no one came, he would deliberately open the gate himself, which he could do perfectly well, and let himself out. In twenty minutes or so he would be back at the gate and barking for admission once more, and finally, if no one paid any attention, letting himself in.

Dandy always had something to eat at meal-times, but he too liked a snack between meals once or twice a day. The dog-biscuits were kept in an open box on the lower dresser shelf, so that he could get one "whenever he felt so disposed," but he didn't like the trouble this arrangement gave him, so he would sit down and start barking, and as he had a bark which was both deep and loud, after it had been repeated a dozen times at intervals of five seconds, any person who happened to be in or near the kitchen was glad to give him his biscuit for the sake of peace and quietness. If no one gave it to him, he would then take it out himself and eat it.

Now it came to pass that during the last year of the war dog-biscuits, like many other articles of food for man and beast, grew scarce, and were finally not to be had at all. At all events, that was what happened in Dandy's town of Penzance. He missed his biscuits greatly and often reminded us of it by barking; then, lest we should think he was barking about something else, he would go and sniff and paw at the empty box. He perhaps thought it was pure forgetfulness on the part of those of the house who went every morning to do the marketing and had fallen into the habit of returning without dog-biscuits in the basket. One day during that last winter of scarcity and anxiety I went to the kitchen and found the floor strewn all over with the fragments of Dandy's biscuit-box. Dandy himself had done it; he had dragged the box from its place out into the middle of the floor, and then deliberately set himself to bite and tear it into small pieces and scatter them about. He was caught at it just as he was finishing the job, and the kindly person who surprised him in the act suggested that the reason of his breaking up the box in that way was that he got something of the biscuit flavor by biting the pieces. My own theory was that as the box was there to hold biscuits and now held none, he had come to regard it as useless—as having lost its function, so to speak—also that its presence there was an insult to his intelligence, a constant temptation to make a fool of himself by visiting it half a dozen times a day only to find it empty as usual. Better, then, to get rid of it altogether, and no doubt when he did it he put a little temper into the business!

Dandy, from the time I first knew him, was strictly teetotal, but in former and distant days he had been rather fond of his glass. If a person held up a glass of beer before him, I was told, he wagged his tail in joyful anticipation, and a little beer was always given him at mealtime. Then he had an experience, which, after a little hesitation, I have thought it best to relate, as it is perhaps the most curious incident in Dandy's somewhat uneventful life.

One day Dandy, who after the manner of his kind, had attached himself to the person who was always willing to take him out for a stroll, followed his friend to a neighboring public-house, where the said friend

had to discuss some business matter with the landlord. They went into the taproom, and Dandy, finding that the business was going to be a rather long affair, settled himself down to have a nap. Now it chanced that a barrel of beer which had just been broached had a leaky tap, and the landlord had set a basin on the floor to catch the waste. Dandy, waking from his nap and hearing the trickling sound, got up, and going to the basin quenched his thirst, after which he resumed his nap. By-and-by he woke again and had a second drink, and altogether he woke and had a drink five or six times; then, the business being concluded, they went out together, but no sooner were they out in the fresh air than Dandy began to exhibit signs of inebriation. He swerved from side to side, colliding with the passers-by, and finally fell off the pavement into the swift stream of water which at that point runs in the gutter at one side of the street. Getting out of the water, he started again, trying to keep close to the wall to save himself from another ducking. People looked curiously at him, and by-and-by they began to ask what the matter was. "Is your dog going to have a fit—or what is it?" they asked. Dandy's friend said he didn't know; something was the matter, no doubt, and he would take him home as quickly as possible and see to it.

When they finally got to the house Dandy staggered to the sofa, and succeeded in climbing on to it and, throwing himself on his cushion, went fast to sleep, and slept on without a break until the following morning. Then he rose quite refreshed and appeared to have forgotten all about it; but that day when at dinner-time some one said "Dandy" and help up a glass of beer, instead of wagging his tail as usual he dropped it between his legs and turned away in evident disgust. And from that time onward he would never touch it with his tongue, and it was plain that when they tried to tempt him, setting beer before him and smilingly inviting him to drink, he knew they were mocking him, and before turning away he would emit a low growl and show his teeth. It was the one thing that put him out and would make him angry with his friends and life companions.

I should not have related this incident if Dandy had been alive. But he is no longer with us. He was old—half-way between fifteen and sixteen: it seemed as though he had waited to see the end of the war, since no sooner was the armistice proclaimed than he began to decline rapidly. Gone deaf and blind, he still insisted on taking several constitutionals every day, and would bark as usual at the gate, and if no one came to let him out or admit him, he would open it for himself as before. This went on till January, 1919, when some of the boys he knew were coming back to Penzance and to the house. Then he established

himself on his sofa, and we knew that his end was near, for there he would sleep all day and all night, declining food. It is customary in this country to chloroform a dog and give him a dose of strychnine to "put him out of his misery." But it was not necessary in this case, as he was not in misery; not a groan did he ever emit, walking or sleeping; and if you put a hand on him he would look up and wag his tail just to let you know that it was well with him. And in his sleep he passed away—a perfect case of euthanasia —and was buried in the large garden near the second apple-tree.

Jane Welsh Carlyle

1801-1866

LETTER FROM
"NERO" TO
THOMAS CARLYLE

Tuesday Jan. 29th, 1850

Dear Master, I take the liberty to write to you myself (my mistress being out of the way of writing to you she says) that you may know Columbine [*the cat*] and I are quite well, and play about as usual. There was no dinner yesterday to speak of; I had for my share only a piece of biscuit that might have been round the world; and if Columbine got anything at all, I didn't see it. I made a grab at one of two 'small beings' on my mistress's plate; she called them heralds of the morn; but my mistress said, 'Don't you wish you may get it?' and boxed my ears. I wasn't taken to walk on account of its being wet. And nobody came, but a man for a 'burial rate'; and my mistress gave him a rowing, because she wasn't going to be buried here at all. Columbine and I don't mind where we are buried.

Tuesday evening.

Dear Master, My mistress brought my chain, and said 'come along with me, while it shined, and I could finish after.' But she kept me so long in the London Library, and other places, that I had to miss the post.

Wednesday.

I left off, last night, dear master, to be washed. This morning I have seen a note from you, which says you will come tomorrow. Columbine and I am extremely happy to hear it; for then there will be some dinner to come and go on. Being to see you so soon, no more at present from your

Obedient little dog,
Nero.

Mark Twain
1835-1910

THE PINCHBUG AND
THE POODLE

The minister made a grand and moving picture of the assembling together of the world's hosts at the millennium when the lion and the lamb should lie down together and a little child should lead them. But the pathos, the lesson, the moral of the great spectacle were lost upon the boy; he only thought of the conspicuousness of the principal character before the onlooking nations; his face lit with the thought, and he said to himself that he wished he could be that child, if it was a tame lion.

Now he lapsed into suffering again, as the dry argument was resumed. Presently he bethought him of a treasure he had and got it out. It was a large black beetle with formidable jaws—a "pinchbug," he

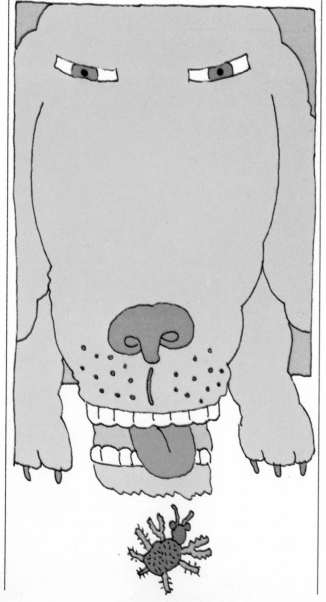

called it. It was in a percussion-cap box. The first thing the beetle did was to take him by the finger. A natural fillip followed, the beetle went floundering into the aisle and lit on its back, and the hurt finger went into the boy's mouth. The beetle lay there working its helpless legs, unable to turn over. Tom eyed it, and longed for it; but it was safe out of his reach. Other people uninterested in the sermon, found relief in the beetle, and they eyed it too. Presently a vagrant poodle-dog came idling along, sad at heart, lazy with the summer softness and the quiet, weary of captivity, sighing for change. He spied the beetle; the drooping tail lifted and wagged. He surveyed the prize; walked around it; smelt at it from a safe distance; walked around it again; grew bolder, and took a closer smell; then lifted his lip and made a gingerly snatch at it, just missing it; made another, and another; began to enjoy the diversion; subsided to his stomach with the beetle between his paws, and continued his experiments; grew weary at last, and then indifferent and absent-minded. His head nodded, and little by little his chin descended and touched the enemy, who seized it. There was a sharp yelp, a flirt of the poodle's head, and the beetle fell a couple of yards away, and lit on its back once more. The neighboring spectators shook with a gentle inward joy, several faces went behind fans and handkerchiefs, and Tom was entirely happy. The dog looked foolish, and probably felt so; but there was resentment in his heart, too, and a craving for revenge. So he went to the beetle and began a wary attack on it again; jumping at it from every point of a circle, lighting with his fore paws within an inch of the creature, making even closer snatches at it with his teeth, and jerking his head till his ears flapped again. But he grew tired once more, after a while; tried to amuse himself with a fly but found no relief; followed an ant around, with his nose close to the floor, and quickly wearied of that; yawned, sighed, forgot the beetle entirely, and sat down on it. Then there was a wild yelp of agony and the poodle went sailing up the aisle; the yelps continued, and so did the dog; he crossed the house in front of the altar; he flew down the other aisle; he crossed before the doors; he clamored up the homestretch; his anguish grew with his progress, till presently he was but a woolly comet moving in its orbit with the gleam and the speed of light. At last the frantic sufferer sheered from its course, and sprang into its master's lap; he flung it out of the window, and the voice of distress quickly thinned away and died in the distance.

By this time the whole church was red-faced and suffocating with suppressed laughter, and the sermon had come to a dead standstill.

THE HOUND PUP

We four always spread our common stock of blankets together on the frozen ground, and slept side by side; and finding that our foolish, long-legged hound pup had a deal of animal heat in him, Okiphant got to admitting him to the bed, between himself and Mr. Ballou, hugging the dog's warm back to his breast and finding great comfort in it. But in the night the pup would get stretchy and brace his feet against the old man's back and shove, grunting complacently the while; and now and then, being warm and snug, grateful and happy, he would paw the old man's back simply in excess of comfort; and at yet other times he would dream of the chase and in his sleep tug at the old man's back hair and bark in his ear. The old gentleman complained mildly about these familiarities, at last, and when he got through with his statement he said that such a dog as that was not a proper animal to admit to bed with tired men, because he was "so meretricious in his movements and so organic in his emotions." We turned the dog out.

THE DINGO

I also saw the wild Australian dog—the dingo. He was a beautiful creature—shapely, graceful, a little wolfish in some of his aspects, but with a most friendly eye and sociable disposition. The dingo is not an importation; he was present in great force when the whites first came to the continent. It may be that he is the oldest dog in the universe; his origin, his descent, the place where his ancestors first appeared, are as unknown and as untraceable as are the camel's. He is the most precious dog in the world, for he does not bark. But in an evil hour he got to raiding the sheep-runs to appease his hunger, and that sealed his doom. He is hunted, now, just as if he were a wolf. He has been sentenced to extermination, and the sentence will be carried out. This is all right, and not objectionable. The world was made for man—the white man.

THE IRON DOG

The drunken man reeled toward home late at night; made a mistake and entered the wrong gate; thought he saw a dog on the stoop; and it was—an iron one. He stopped and considered; wondered if it was a dangerous dog; ventured to say "Be (hic!) begone!" No effect. Then he approached warily, and adopted conciliation; pursed up his lips and tried to whistle, but failed; still approached, saying, "Poor dog!—doggy, doggy, doggy!—poor doggy-dog!" Got up on the stoop, still petting with fond names, till master of the advantages; then exclaimed, "Leave, you thief!"—planted a vindictive kick in his ribs, and went head-over-heels overboard, of course. A pause; a sigh or two of pain, and then a remark in a reflective voice:

"Awful solid dog. What could he b'en eating? ('ic!) Rocks, p'raps. Such animals is dangerous. 'At's what *I* say—they're dangerous. If a man—('ic!)—if a man wants to feed a dog on rocks, let him *feed* him on rocks; 'at's all right; but let him keep him at *home*—not have him layin' round promiscuous, where ('ic!) where people's liable to stumble over him when they ain't noticin'!"

THE DACHSHUND

In the train, during a part of the return journey from Baroda, we had the company of a gentleman who had with him a remarkable-looking dog. I had not seen one of its kind before, as far as I could remember; though of course I might have seen one and not noticed it, for I am not acquainted with dogs, but only with cats. This dog's coat was smooth and shiny and black, and I think it had tan trimmings around the edges of the dog, and perhaps underneath. It was a long, low dog, with very short, strange legs—legs that curved inboard, something like parentheses turned the wrong way (. Indeed, it was made on the plan of a bench for length and lowness. It seemed to be satisfied, but I thought the plan poor, and structurally weak, on account of the distance between the forward supports and those abaft. With age the dog's back was likely to sag; and it seemed to me that it would have been a stronger and more practicable dog it if had had some more legs. It had not begun to sag yet, but the shape of the legs showed that the undue weight imposed upon them was beginning to tell. It had a long nose, and floppy ears that hung down, and a resigned expression of countenance. I did not like to ask what kind of a dog it was, or how it came to be deformed, for it was plain that the gentleman was very fond of it, and naturally he could be sensitive about it. From delicacy I thought it best not to seem to notice it too much. No doubt a man with a dog like that feels just as a person does who has a child that is out of true. The gentleman was not merely fond of the dog, he was also proud of it—just the same, again, as a mother feels about her child when it is an idiot. I could see that he was proud of it, notwithstanding it was such a long dog and looked so resigned and pious. It had been all over the world with him, and had been pilgriming like that for years and years. It had traveled fifty thousand miles by sea and rail, and had ridden in front of him on his horse eight thousand. It had a silver medal from the Geographical Society of Great Britain for its travels, and I saw it. It had won prizes in dog-shows, both in India and in England—I saw them.

He said its pedigree was on record in the Kennel Club, and that it was a well-known dog. He said a great many people in London could recognize it the moment they saw it. I did not say anything, but I did not think it anything strange; I should know that dog again, myself, yet I am not careful about noticing dogs. He said that when he walked along in London, people often stopped and looked at the dog. Of course I did not say anything, for I did not want to hurt his feelings, but I could have explained to him that if you take a great long low dog like that and waddle it along the street anywhere in the world and not charge anything, people will stop and look. He was gratified because the dog took prizes. But that was nothing; if I were built like that I could take prizes myself. I wished I knew what kind of a dog it was, and what it was for, but I could not very well ask, for that would show that I did not know. Not that I want a dog like that, but only to know the secret of its birth.

I think he was going to hunt elephants with it, because I know, from remarks dropped by him, that he has hunted large game in India and Africa, and likes it. But I think that if he tries to hunt elephants with it, he is going to be disappointed. I do not believe that it is suited for elephants. It lacks energy, it lacks force of character, it lacks bitterness. These things all show in the meekness and resignation of its expression. It would not attack an elephant, I am sure of it. It might not run if it saw one coming, but it looked to me like a dog that would sit down and pray.

UNCLE LEM'S COMPOSITE DOG

You look at my Uncle Lem—what do you say to that? That's all I ask you—you just look at my Uncle Lem and talk to me about accidents! It was like this: one day my Uncle Lem and his dog was downtown, and he was a-leaning up against a scaffolding—sick, or drunk, or somethin'—and there was an Irishman with a hod of bricks up the ladder along about the third story, and his foot slipped and down he come, bricks and all, and hit a stranger fair and square and knocked the everlasting aspirations out of him; he was ready for the coroner in two minutes. Now them people said it was an accident.

"Accident! there warn't no accident about it; 'twas a special providence, and had a mysterious, noble intention back of it. The idea was to save that Irishman. If the stranger hadn't been there that Irishman would have been killed. The people said 'special providence—sho! the dog was there—why didn't the Irishman fall on the dog? Why warn't the dog app'inted?' Fer a mightly good reason—the dog would 'a' seen him a-coming; you can't depend on no dog to carry out a special providence. You couldn't hit a dog with an Irishman because—lemme see, what was that dog's name…(musing) …oh, yes, Jasper—and a mighty good dog too; he wa'n't no common dog, he wa'n't no mongrel; he was a composite. A composite dog is a dog that's made up of all the valuable qualities that's in the dog breed—kind of a syndicate; and a mongrel is made up of the riffraff that's left over. That Jasper was one of the most wonderful dogs you ever see. Uncle Lem got him off the Wheelers. I reckon you've heard of the Wheelers; ain't no better blood south of the line than the Wheelers."

Every dog must have his day.   *Swift*

Rudyard Kipling

1865-1936

GARM—
A HOSTAGE

One night, a very long time ago, I drove to an Indian military encampment called Mian Mir to see amateur theatricals. At the back of the Infantry barracks a soldier, his cap over one eye, rushed in front of the horses and shouted that he was a dangerous highway robber. As a matter of fact, he was a friend of mine, so I told him to go home before any one caught him; but he fell under the pole, and I heard voices of a military guard in search of some one.

The driver and I coaxed him into the carriage, drove home swiftly, undressed him and put him to bed, where he waked next morning with a sore headache, very much ashamed. When his uniform was cleaned and dried, and he had been shaved and washed and made neat, I drove him back to barracks with his arm in a fine white sling, and reported that I had accidentally run over him. I did not tell this story to my friend's sergeant, who was a hostile and unbelieving person, but to his lieutenant, who did not know us quite so well.

Three days later my friend came to call, and at his heels slobbered and fawned one of the finest bull-terriers—of the old-fashioned breed, two parts bull and one terrier—that I had ever set eyes on. He was pure white, with a fawn-colored saddle just behind his neck, and a fawn diamond at the root of his thin whippy tail. I had admired him distantly for more than a year; and Vixen, my own fox-terrier, knew him too, but did not approve.

"'E's for you," said my friend; but he did not look as though he liked parting with him.

"Nonsense! That dog's worth more than most men, Stanley," I said.

"'E's that and more. 'Tention!"

The dog rose on his hind legs, and stood upright for a full minute.

"Eyes right!"

He sat on his haunches and turned his head sharp to the right. At a sign he rose and barked twice. Then he shook hands with his right paw and bounded lightly to my shoulder. Here he made himself into a necktie, limp and lifeless, hanging down on either side of my neck. I was told to pick him up and throw him in the air. He fell with a howl and held up one leg.

"Part o' the trick," said his owner. "You're going to die now. Dig yourself your little grave an' shut your little eye."

Still limping, the dog hobbled to the garden edge, dug a hole and lay down in it. When told that he was cured, he jumped out, wagging his tail, and whining for applause. He was put through half a dozen other tricks, such as showing how he would hold a man safe (I was that man, and he sat down before me, his teeth bared, ready to spring), and how he would stop eating at the word of command. I had no more than finished praising him when my friend made a gesture that stopped the dog as though he had been shot, took a piece of blue-ruled canteen-paper from his helmet, handed it to me and ran away, while the dog looked after him and howled. I read:

Sir—I give you the dog because of what you got me out of. He is the best I know, for I made him myself, and he is as good as a man. Please do not give him too much to eat, and please do not give him back to me, for I'm not going to take him, if you will keep him. So please do not try to give him back any more. I have kept his name back, so you can call him anything and he will answer, but please do not give him back. He can kill a man as easy as anything, but please do not give him too much meat. He knows more than a man.

Vixen sympathetically joined her shrill yap to the bull-terrier's despairing cry, and I was annoyed, for I knew that a man who cares for dogs is one thing, but a man who loves one dog is quite another. Dogs are at the best no more than verminous vagrants, self-scratchers, foul feeders, and unclean by the law of Moses and Mohammed; but a dog with whom one lives alone for a least six months in the year; a free thing, tied to you so strictly by love that without you he will not stir or exercise; a patient, temperate, humorous, wise soul, who knows your moods before you know them yourself, is not a dog under any ruling.

I had Vixen, who was all my dog to me; and I felt what my friend must have felt, at tearing out his heart in this style and leaving it in my garden.

However, the dog understood clearly enough that I was his master, and did not follow the soldier. As soon as he drew breath I made much of him, and Vixen, yelling with jealousy, flew at him. Had she been of his own sex, he might have cheered himself with a fight, but he only looked worriedly when she nipped his deep iron sides, laid his heavy head on my knee, and howled anew. I meant to dine at the Club that night, but as darkness drew in, and the dog snuffed through the empty house like a child trying to recover from a fit of sobbing, I felt that I could not leave him to suffer his first evening alone. So we fed at home, Vixen on one side, and the stranger-dog on the other; she watching his every mouthful, and saying explicitly what thought of his table manners, which were better than hers.

There was one corner of a village near by, which we generally pass with caution, because all the yellow pariah dogs of the place gathered about it. They were half-wild, starving beasts, and though utter cowards, yet where nine or ten of them get together they will mob and kill and eat an English dog. I kept a whip with a long lash for them. That morning they attacked Vixen, who, perhaps of design, had moved from beyond my horse's shadow.

The bull was ploughing along in the dust, fifty yards behind, rolling in his run, and smiling as bull terriers will. I heard Vixen squeal; half a dozen of the curs closed in on her; a white streak came up behind me; a cloud of dust rose near Nixen, and, when it cleared, I saw one tall pariah with his back broken, and the bull wrenching another to earth. Vixen retreated to the protection of my whip, and the bull padded back smiling more than ever, covered with the blood of his enemies. That decided me to call him "Garm of the Bloody Breast," who was a great person in his time, or "Garm" for short; so, leaning forward, I told him what his temporary name would be. He looked up while I repeated it, and then raced away. I shouted "Garm!" He stopped, raced back, and came up to ask my will.

But the long days in my office tried him sorely. We three would drive off in the morning at half-past eight and come home at six or later. Vixen, knowing the routine of it, went to sleep under my table; but the confinement ate into Garm's soul. He generally sat on the veranda looking out on the Mall; and well I knew what he expected.

Sometimes a company of soldiers would move along on their way to the Fort, and Garm rolled forth to inspect them; or an officer in uniform entered into the office, and it was pitiful to see poor Gram's welcome to the cloth—not the man. He would leap at him, and sniff and bark joyously, then run to the door and back again. One afternoon I heard him bay with a full throat—a thing I had never heard before—and he disappeared. When I drove into my garden at the end of the day a soldier in white uniform scrambled over the wall at the far end, and the Garm that met me was a joyous dog. This happened twice or thrice a week for a month.

I pretended not to notice, but Garm knew and Vixen knew. He would glide homewards from the office about four o'clock, as though he were only going to look at the scenery, and this he did so quietly that but for Vixen I should not have noticed him. The jealous little dog under the table would give a sniff and a snort, just loud enough to call my attention to the flight. Garm might go out forty times in the day and Vixen would never stir, but when he slunk off to see his true master in my garden she told me in her own tongue. That was the one sign she made to prove the Garm did not altogether belong to the family. They were the best of friends at all times, *but,* Vixen explained that I was never to forget Garm did not love me as she loved me.

I never expected it. The dog was not my dog—could never be my dog—and I knew he was as miserable as his master who tramped eight miles a day to see him. So it seemed to me that the sooner the two were reunited the better for all. One afternoon I sent Vixen home alone in the dog-cart (Garm had gone before), and rode over to cantonments to find another friend of mine, who was an Irish soldier and a great friend of the dog's master.

I explained the whole case, and wound up with:

"And now Stanley's in my garden crying over his dog. Why doesn't he take him back? They're both unhappy."

"Unhappy! There's no sense in the little man any more. But 'tis his fit."

"What *is* his fit? He travels fifty miles a week to see the brute, and he pretends not to notice me when he sees me on the road; and I'm as unhappy as he is. Make him take the dog back."

"It's his penance he's set himself. I told him by way of a joke, afther you'd run over him so convenient that night, whin he was drunk—I said if he was a Catholic he'd do penance. Off he went wid that fit in his little head *an'* a dose of fever, an' nothin' would suit but givin' you the dog as a hosage."

"Hostage for what? I don't want hostages from Stanley."

"For his good behaviour. He's keepin' straight now, the way it's no pleasure to associate wid him."

"Has he taken the pledge?"

"If 'twas only that I need not care. Ye can take the pledge for three months on an' off. He sez he'll never see the dog again, an' *so* mark you, he'll keep straight for evermore. Ye know his fits? Well, this is wan of them. How's the dog takin' it?"

"Like a man. He's the best dog in India. Can't you make Stanley take him back?"

"I can do no more than I have done. But ye know his fits. He's just doin' his penance. What will he do when he goes to the Hills? The docthor's put him on the list."

It is the custom in India to send a certain number of invalids from each regiment up to stations in the Himalayas for the hot weather; and though the men ought to enjoy the cool and the comfort, they

miss the society of the barracks down below, and do their best to come back or to avoid going. I felt that this move would bring matters to a head, so I left Terrence hopefully, though he called after me:

"He won't take the dog, sorr. You can lay your month's pay on that. Ye know his fits."

I never pretended to understand Private Ortheris, and so I did the next best thing—I left him alone.

That summer the invalids of the regiment to which my friend belonged were ordered off to the Hills early, because the doctors thought marching in cool of the day would do them good. Their route lay south to a place called Umballa, a hundred and twenty miles or more. Then they would turn east and march up into the Hills to Kasauli or Dugshai or Subathoo. I dined with the officers the night before they left—they were marching at five in the morning. It was midnight when I drove into my garden, and surprised a white-figure flying over the wall.

"That man," said my butler, "has been here since nine, making talk to that dog. He is quite mad. I did not tell him to go away because he has been here many times before, and because the dog-boy told me that if I told him to go away, that great dog would immediately slay me. He did not wish to speak to the Protector of the Poor, and he did not ask for anything to eat or drink."

"Kadir Buksh," said I, "that was well done, for the dog would surely have killed thee. But I do not think the white soldier will come any more."

Garm slept ill that night and whimpered in his dreams. Once he sprang up with a clear, ringing bark, and I heard him wag his tail till it waked him and the bark died out in a howl. He dreamed he was with his master again, and I nearly cried. It was all Stanley's fault.

The first halt which the detachment of invalids made was some miles from their barracks, on the Amritsar road, and ten miles distant from my house. By a mere chance one of the officers drove back for another good dinner at the Club (cooking on the line of march is always bad), and there we met. He as a particular friend of mine, and I knew that he knew how to love a dog properly. His pet was a big retriever who was going up to the Hills for his health, and, though it was still April, the round, brown brute puffed and panted in the Club veranda as though he would burst.

"It's amazing," said the officer, "what excuses these invalids of mine make to get back to barracks. There's a man in my company now asked me for leave to go back to cantonments to pay a debt he'd forgotten. I was so taken by the idea I let him go,

and he jingled off in an *ekka* as pleased as Punch. Ten miles to pay a debt. Wonder what it was really?"

"If you'll drive me home I think I can show you," I said.

So he went over to my house in his dog-cart with the retriever; and on the way I told him the story of Garm.

"I was wondering where that brute had gone to. He's the best dog in the regiment," said my friend. "I offered the little fellow twenty rupees for him a month ago. But he's a hostage, you say, for Stanley's good conduct. Stanley's one of the best men I have —when he chooses."

"That's the reason why," I said. "A second-rate man wouldn't have taken things to heart as he has done."

We drove in quietly at the far end of the garden, and crept round the house. There was a place close to the wall all grown about with tamarisk trees, where I knew Garm kept his bones. Even Vixen was not allowed to sit near it. In the full Indian moonlight I could see a white uniform bending over the dog.

"Good-bye, old man," we could not help hearing Stanley's voice. "For 'Eving's sake don't get bit and go mad by any measley pi-dog. But you can look after yourself, old man. *You* don't get drunk an' run about 'ittin' your friends. You takes your bones an' eats your biscuit, an' kills your enemy like a gentleman. I'm goin' away—don't 'owl—I'm goin' off to Kasauli, where I won't see you no more."

I could hear him holding Garm's nose as the dog drew it up to the stars.

"You'll stay here an' be'ave, an'—an' I'll go away an' try to be', an' I don't know 'ow to leave you. I don't think—"

"I think this is damn silly," said the officer, patting his foolish fubsy old retriever. He called to the private who leaped to his feet, marched forward, and saluted.

"You here?" said the officer, turning away his head.

"Yes, sir, but I'm just goin' back."

"I shall be leaving here at eleven in my cart. You come with me. I can't have sick men running about all over the place. Report yourself at eleven, *here*."

We did not say much when we went indoors, but the officer muttered and pulled his retriever's ears.

He was a disgraceful, overfed doormat of a dog; and when he waddled off to my cookhouse to be fed, I had a brilliant idea.

At eleven o'clock that officer's dog was nowhere to be found, and you never heard such a fuss as his owner made. He called and shouted and grew angry, and hunted through my garden for half an hour.

Then I said:

"He's sure to turn up in the morning. Send a man in by rail, and I'll find the beast and return him."

"Beast?" said the officer. "I value that dog considerably more than I value any man I know. It's all very fine for you to talk—your dog's here."

So she was—under my feet—and, had she been missing, food and wages would have stopped in my house till her return. But some people grow fond of dogs not worth a cut of the whip. My friend had to drive away at last with Stanley in the back seat; and then the dog-boy said to me:

"What kind of animal is Bullen Sahib's dog? Look at him!"

I went to the boy's hut, and the fat old reprobate was lying on a mat carefully chained up. He must have heard his master calling for twenty minutes, but had not even attempted to join him.

"He has no face," said the dog-boy scornfully. "He is a *punniarkooter* [a spaniel]. He never tried to get that cloth off his jaws when his master called. Now Vixen-baba would have jumped through the window, and that Great Dog would have slain me with his muzzled mouth. It is true that there are many kinds of dogs."

Next evening who should turn up but Stanley. The officer had sent him back fourteen miles by rail with a note begging me to return the retriever if I had found him, and, if I had not, to offer huge rewards. The last train to camp left at half-past ten, and Stanley stayed till ten talking to Garm. I argued and entreated, and even threatened to shoot the bull-terrier, but the little man was firm as a rock, though I gave him a good dinner and talked to him most severely. Garm knew as well as I that this was the last time he could hope to see his man, and followed Stanley like a shadow. The retriever said nothing, but licked his lips after his meal and waddled off without so much as saying "Thank you" to the disgusted dog-boy.

So that last meeting was over, and I felt as wretched as Garm, who moaned in his sleep all night. When we went to the office he found a place under the table close to Vixen, and dropped flat till it was time to go home. There was no more running out into the verandas, no slinking away for stolen talks with Stanley. As the weather grew warmer the dogs were forbidden to run beside the cart, but sat at my side of the seat. Vixen with her head under the crook of my left elbow, and Garm hugging the left handrail.

Once, and only once, did I see Garm at all contented with his surrounding. He had gone for an unauthorized walk with Vixen early one Sunday morning, and a very young and foolish artilleryman (his battery had just moved to that part of the world) tried to steal both. Vixen, of course, knew better than to take food from soldiers, and, beside, she had just finished her breakfast. So she trotted back with

a large piece of mutton that they issue to our troops, laid it down on my veranda, and looked up to see what I thought. I asked her where Garm was, and she ran in front of the house to show me the way.

About a mile up the road we came across our artilleryman sitting very stiffly on the edge of a culvert with a greasy handkerchief on his knees. Garm was in front of him, looking rather pleased. When the man moved leg or hand, Garm bared his teeth in silence. A broken string hung from his collar, and the other half of it lay, all warm, in the artilleryman's still hand. He explained to me, keeping his eye straight in front of him, that he had met this dog (he called him awful names) walking alone, and was going to take him to the Fort to be killed for a masterless pariah.

I said that Garm did not seem to me much of a pariah, but that he had better take him to the Fort if he thought best. He said he did not care to do so. I told him to go to the Fort alone. He said he did not want to go at that hour, but would follow my advice as soon as I had called off the dog. I instructed Garm to take him to the Fort, and Garm marched him solemnly up to the gate, one mile and a half under a hot sun, and I told the quarter-guard what had happened; but the young artrilleryman was more angry than was at all necessary when they began to laugh. Several regiments, he was told, had tried to steal Garm in their time.

That month the hot weather shut down in earnest, and the dogs slept in the bathroom on the cool wet bricks where the bath is placed. Every morning, as soon as the man filled my bath, the two jumped in, and every morning the man filled the bath a second time. I said to him that he might as well fill a small tub especially for the dogs. "Nay," said he smiling, "it is not their custom. They would not understand. Besides, the big bath gives them more space."

Living with the dog as I did, I never noticed that he was more than ordinarily upset by the hot weather, till one day at the Club a man said: "That dog of yours will die in a week or two. He's a shadow." Then I dosed Garm with iron and quinine, which he hated; and I felt very anxious. He lost his appetite, and Vixen was allowed to eat his dinner under his eyes. Even that did not make him swallow, and we held a consultation on him, of the best man-doctor in the place; a lady-doctor, who had cured sick wives of kings; and the Deputy Inspector-General of the veterinary service of all India. They pronounced upon his symptoms, and I told them his story, and Garm lay on a sofa licking my hand.

"He's dying of a broken heart," said the lady-doctor suddenly.

" 'Pon my word," said the Deputy Inspector-General, "I believe Mrs. Macrae is perfectly right—

as usual."

The best man-doctor in the place wrote a prescription, and the veterinary Deputy Inspector-General went over it afterwards to be sure that the drugs were in the proper dog-proportions; and that was the first time in his life that our doctor ever allowed his prescriptions to be edited. It was a strong tonic, and it put the dear boy on his feet for a week or two; then he lost flesh again. I asked a man I knew to take him up to the Hills with him when he went, and the man came to the door with his kit packed on the top of the carriage. Garm took in the situation at one red glance. The hair rose along his back; he sat down in front of me, and delivered the most awful growl I have ever heard in the jaws of a dog. I shouted to my friend to get away at once, and as soon as the carriage was out of the garden Garm laid his head on my knee and whined. So I knew his answer, and devoted myself to getting Stanley's address in the Hills.

My turn to go to the cool came late in August. We were allowed thirty days' holiday in a year, if one fell sick, and we took it as we could be spared. My chief and Bob the Librarian had their holiday first, and when they were gone I made a calendar, as I always did, and hung it up at the head of my cot, tearing off one day at a time till they returned. Vixen had gone up to the Hills with me five times before; and she appreciated the cold and the damp and the beautiful wood fires there as much as I did.

"Garm," I said, "we are going back to Stanley at Kasauli. Kasauli—Stanley; Stanley-Kasauli." And I repeated it twenty times. It was not Kasauli really, but another place. Still I remembered what Stanley had said in my garden on the last night, and I dared not change the name. Then Garm began to tremble; then he barked; and then he leaped up at me, frisking and wagging his tail.

"Not now," I said, holding up my hand. "When I say 'Go', we'll go, Garm." I pulled out the little blanket coat and spiked collar that Vixen always wore up in the Hills to protect her against sudden chills and theiving leopards, and I let the two smell them and talk it over. What they said of course I do not know, but it made a new dog of Garm. His eyes were bright; and he barked joyfully when I spoke to him. He ate his food, and he killed his rats for the next three weeks, and when he began to whine I had only to say "Stanley—Kasauli; Kasauli—Stanley," to wake him up. I wish I had thought of it before.

My chief came back, all brown with living in the open air, and very angry at finding it so hot in the Plains. That same afternoon we three and Kadir Buksh began to pack for our month's holiday, Vixen rolling in and out of the bullock-trunk twenty times a minute, and Garm grinning all over and thumping on the floor with his tail. Vixen knew the routine of travelling as well as she knew my office-work. She went to the station, singing songs, on the front seat of the carriage, while Garm sat with me. She hurried into the railway carriage, saw Kadir Buksh make up my bed for the night, got her drink of water, and curled up with her black-patch eye on the tumult of the platform. Garm followed her (the crowd gave him a lane all to himself) and sat down on the pillows with his eyes blazing, and his tail a haze behind him.

We came to Umballa in the hot misty dawn, four or five men, who had been working hard for eleven months, shouting for our daks—the two-horse travelling carriages that were to take us up to Kalka at the foot of the Hills.

After Kalka the road wound among the Hills, and we took a curricle with half-broken ponies, which were changed every six miles. Here, again, Vixen led Garm from one carriage to the other; jumped into the back seat and shouted. A cool breath from the snows met us about five miles out of Kalka, and she whined for her coat, wisely fearing a chill on the liver. I had had one made for Garm too, and, as we climbed to the fresh breezes, I put it on, and Garm chewed it uncomprehendingly, but I think he was grateful.

"Hi-yi-yi-yi!" sang Vixen as we shot around the curves; "Toot-toot-toot!" went the driver's bugle at the dangerous places, and "Yow! Yow! Yow! Yow!" bayed Garm. Kadir Buksh sat on the front seat and smiled. Even he was glad to get away from the heat of the Plains that stewed in the haze behind us. Now and then we would meet a man we knew going down to his work again, and he would say: "What's it like below?" and I would shout: "Hotter than cinders. What's it like above?" and he would shout back: "Just perfect!" and away we would go.

Suddenly Kadir Buksh said, over his shoulder: "Here is Solon;" and Garm snored where he lay with his head on my knee. Solon is an unpleasant little cantonment, but it has the advantage of being cool and healthy. It is all bare and windy, and one generally stops at a rest-house near by for something to eat. I got out and took both dogs with me, while Kadir Buksh made tea. A soldier told us we should find Stanley "out there," nodding his head towards a bare, bleak hill.

When we climbed to the top we spied that very Stanley, who had given me all this trouble, sitting on a rock with his face in his hands, and his overcoat hanging loose about him. I never saw anything so lonely and dejected in my life as this one little man crumpled up and thinking, on the great gray hillside. Here Garm left me.

He departed without a word, and, so far as I could see, without moving his legs. He flew through the air bodily, and I heard the whack of him as he flung himself at Stanley, knocking the little man clean over. They rolled on the ground together, shouting, and yelping, and hugging. I could not see which was dog and which was man, till Stanley got up and whimpered.

He told me that he had been suffering from fever at intervals, and was very weak. He looked all he said, but even while I watched, both man and dog plumped out to their natural sizes, precisely as dried apples swell in water, Garm was on his shoulder, and his breast and feet all at the same time, so that Stanley spoke all through a cloud of Garm—gulping, sobbing, slavering Garm. He did not say anything that I could understand, except that he had fancied he was going to die, but that now he was quite well, and that he was not going to give up Garm any more to anybody under the rank of Beelzebub.

Then he said he felt hungry, and thirsty, and happy.

We went down to tea at the rest-house, where Stanley stuffed himself with sardines and raspberry jam, and beer, and cold mutton and pickles, when Garm wasn't climbing over him; and then Vixen and I went on.

Garm saw how it was at once. He said good-bye to me three times, giving me both paws one after another, and leaping on to my shoulder. He further escorted us, singing Hosannas at the top of his voice, a mile down the road. Then he raced back to his own master.

Vixen never opened her moutn, but when the cold twilight came, and we could see the lights of Simla across the hills, she snuffed with her nose at the breast of my ulster. I unbuttoned it, and tucked her inside. Then she gave a contented little sniff, and fell fast asleep, her head on my breast, till we bundled out of Simla, two of the four happiest people in all the world that night.

Dogs for Defense
1942-

A MESSAGE TO
AMERICA'S
DOG-OWNERS

Total war has made it necessary to call to the colors many of the nation's dogs. Thousands of dogs, donated by patriotic men, women and children and trained for special duties with the Armed Forces, are serving on all fronts as well as standing guard against saboteurs at home.

More thousands of dogs are needed. New recruits are being inducted daily at the War Dog Training Centers, rushed into training courses which skill

them as sentries, message carriers, airplane spotters, pack-carriers—and other tasks which must remain secret. The Army, Navy, Coast Guard and Marines depend on the generosity of the dog owners of the United States to keep that stream of recruits at full flood. They depend on those who own no dogs to speed news of this need to every corner of the land.

Most wanted are dogs of the larger breeds—Belgian Shepherds, Boxers, Airedales, German Shepherds, Doberman Pinschers, Dalmatians, German Short Haired Pointers, Collies, Standard Poodles, Eskimos, Siberian Huskies, St. Bernards, Irish Water Spaniels, Labrador Retrievers, and a dozen others. They must be at least a year old, not more than five. Weight and height requirements vary, according to breed, from 50 pounds to 125 pounds. The animals must be temperamentally suited to military tasks—not gun-shy, not storm-shy. Perfect physical condition is essential.

To register a dog for duty, to learn how to help in the campaign to build up this new unit of the country's military might, communicate at once with the national headquarters of the official dog procurement agency: Dogs for Defense, Inc., 22 East 60th Street, New York, New York.

Men are generally more careful of the breed of their horses and dogs than of their children.

William Penn

If a dog will not come to you after he has looked you in the face, you ought to go home and examine your conscience.

Woodrow Wilson

Jeroslav Hasek

1883-1923

THE GOOD
SOLDIER
SCHWEIK
Excerpts

There's just one thing more, Schweik," said the lieutenant when Schweik was leaving for the post office. "What about that dog you went to look for?"

"I've got my eye on one, sir, and a very fine animal it is, too. But it's going to be a hard job to get hold of him. All the same, I hope I'll manage to bring him along tomorrow. He don't half bite."

Lieutenant Lukash did not hear the last few words, and yet they were very important. "The brute bites for all he's worth," was what Schweik was going to add, but then he thought, "What's it matter to him? He wants a dog, and he'll get one."

Now it is all very well to say, "Get me a dog," but the owners of dogs are very careful of their pets, even though they may not be thoroughbreds. The dog is a faithful animal, but only in schoolbooks or natural history primers. Let even the most faithful dog sniff at a fried sausage and he's done for. He'll forget his master, by whose side he was just trotting along. He'll turn around and follow you, his mouth watering, his tail wagging, his nostrils quivering with gusto in anticipation of the sausage.

The two friends again clinked glasses. It was from Blahnik that Schweik had obtained his supply of dogs when he used to deal in them before joining the army. And now that Schweik was a soldier, Blahnik considered it his duty to assist him in a disinterested spirit. He knew every dog in the whole of Prague and environs, and on principle he stole only thoroughbred dogs.

Blahnik kept his word. In the afternoon, when Schweik had finished tidying up, he heard a barking noise at the door, and when he opened it, Blahnik came in, dragging with him a refractory Pomeranian which was more bristly than his natural bristliness. He was rolling his eyes wildly and his scowl was such that it suggested a starving tiger in a cage being inspected by a well-fed visitor to the Zoological Gardens. He gnashed his teeth and growled, as if expressing his desire to rend and devour.

They tied the dog to the kitchen table, and Blahnik described the procedure by which he had acquired the animal.

"I purposely hung about near him with some boiled liver wrapped up in a piece of paper. He began sniffing and jumping up at me. When I got as far as the park I turns off into Bredovska Street and then I gives him the first bit. He gobbles it up, but keeps on the move all the time so as not to lose sight of me. I turns off into Jindrichska Street and there I gives him another helping. Then, when he'd got that inside him, I puts him on the lead and took him across Vaclav Square to Vinohrady and then on to Vrsovice. And he didn't half lead me a dance. When I was crossing the tram lines he flops down and wouldn't budge an inch. Perhaps he wanted to get run over. I've brought a blank pedigree form that I got at a stationer's shop. You'll have to fill that up, Schweik."

"It's got to be in your handwriting. Say he comes from the Von Bülow kennels at Leipzig. Father, Arnheim von Kahlsberg, mother, Emma von Trautensdorf, and connected with Siegfried von Busenthal on his father's side. Father gained first prize at the Berlin Exhibition of Pomeranians in 1912. Mother awarded a gold medal by the Nürnberg Thoroughbred Dogs' Society. How old do you think he is?"

"Judging by his teeth, I should say two years."

"Put him down as eighteen months."

"He's been badly cropped, Schweik. Look at his ears."

"That can be put right. We can clip them when he's got used to us. He'd show fight if we was to try it now."

The purloined dog growled savagely, panted, wriggled about, and then, tired out, he lay down with tongue hanging out, and waited what would befall him. Gradually he became quieter, only from time to time he whined piteously.

Schweik offered him the rest of the liver which Blahnik had handed over. But he refused to touch it, eyeing it disdainfully and looking at both of them, as much as to say, "I've been had once. Now eat it yourselves."

He lay down with an air of resignation and pretended to be dozing. Then suddenly something flashed across his mind; he got up and began to stand on his hind legs and to beg with his front paws. He had given in.

This touching scene produced no effect on Schweik.

"Lie down," he shouted at the wretched animal, which lay down again, whining piteously.

"What name shall we shove into his pedigree?" asked Blahnik. "He used to be called Fox, or something of that sort."

"Well, let's call him Max. Look how he pricks up his ears. Stand up, Max."

The unfortunate Pomeranian, which had been deprived both of home and name, stood up and awaited further orders.

"I think we might as well untie him," suggested Schweik. "Let's see what he'll do."

When he was untied, the first thing he did was to make for the door, where he gave three short barks at the handle, evidently relying on the magnanimity of these evil people. But when he saw that they did not fall in with his desire to get out, he made a small puddle in the doorway, thinking, most probably, that they would throw him out, as had always happened on similar occasions when he was a puppy and the colonel, with military severity, had taught him elementary manners.

But instead of that, Schweik remarked, "He's an artful one, he is, as artful as they make 'em," gave him a whack with a strap, and wetted his whiskers so thoroughly in the puddle that it was all he could do to lick himself clean.

He whined at this humiliation and began to run about in the kitchen, sniffing desperately at his own tracks. Then, unexpectedly changing his mind, he sat down by the table and devoured the rest of the

liver which was on the floor. Whereupon he lay down by the fireplace and ended his spell of adventure by falling asleep.

"What's the damage?" Schweik asked Blahnik, when he got up to go.

"Don't you worry about that, Schweik," said Blahnik tenderly. "I'd do anything for an old pal, especially when he's in the army. Well, so long, lad, and never take him across Havlicek Square, or you'd be asking for trouble. If you want any more dogs, you know where I hang out."

Schweik let Max have a good long nap. He went to the butcher's and bought half a pound of liver, boiled it, and waited till Max woke up, when he gave him a piece of the warm liver to sniff at. Max began to lick himself after his nap, stretched his limbs, sniffed at the liver, and gulped it down. Then he went to the door and repeated his performance with the handle.

"Max!" shouted Schweik. "Come here."

The dog obeyed gingerly enough, but Schweik took him on his lap and stroked him. Now for the first time since his arrival Max began to wag the remainder of his lopped tail amicably, and playfully grabbed at Schweik's hand, holding it in his paw and gazing at Schweik sagaciously, as much as to say, "Well, it can't be helped; I know I got the worst of it."

Schweik went on stroking him and in a gentle voice began to tell him a little story:

"Now there was once a little dog whose name was Fox, and he lived with a colonel. The servant girl took him for a walk and up came a gentleman who stole Fox. Fox got into the army, where his new master was a lieutenant, and now they called him Max. Max, shake hands. Now you see, you silly tyke, we'll get on well together if you're good and obedient. If you ain't, why, you'll catch it hot."

Max jumped down from Schweik's lap and began to frisk about merrily with him. By the evening, when the lieutenant returned from the barracks, Schweik and Max were the best of friends.

As he looked at Max, Schweik reflected philosophically, "When you come to think of it, every soldier's really been stolen away from his home."

Lieutenant Lukash was very pleasantly surprised when he saw Max, who on his part also showed great joy at again seeing a man with a sword.

When asked where he came from and how much he cost, Schweik replied with the utmost composure that the dog was a present from a friend of his who had just joined up.

"That's fine, Schweik," said the lieutenant, playing with Max. "On the first of the month I'll let you have fifty crowns for the dog."

"I couldn't take the money, sir."

"Schweik," said the lieutenant sternly, "when you entered my service, I explained to you that you must obey me implicity. When I tell you that you'll get fifty crowns, you've got to take the money and go on the spree with it. What will you do with the fifty crown, Schweik?"

"Beg to report, sir, I'll go on the spree with it, as per instructions."

"And if I should happen to forget it, Schweik, you are to remind me to give you the fifty crowns. Do you understand? Are you sure the dog hasn't got fleas? You'd better give him a bath and comb him out. I'm on duty tomorrow, but the day after tomorrow I'll take him for a walk."

While Schweik was giving Max a bath, the colonel, his former owner, was kicking up a terrible row and threatening that when he found the man who had stolen his dog, he would have him tried by court-martial, he would have him shot, he would have him hanged, he would have him imprisoned for twenty years, and he would have him chopped to pieces.

"There'll be hell to pay when I find the blackguard who did it," bellowed the colonel till the windows rattled. "I know how to get even with low scoundrels like him."

Above the heads of Schweik and Lieutenant Lukash was hovering a catastrophe.

Having finished his classwork at the training school for volunteer officers, Lieutenant Lukash went for a walk with Max.

"I hope you don't mind me telling you, sir," said Schweik solicitously, "but you got to be careful with that dog, or he'll run away. I expect he's fretting a bit after his old home, and if you was to untie him, he might take his hook. And if I was you I wouldn't take him across Havlicek Square, because there's a butcher's dog always hanging about around there and he's a terror, he is. The minute he sees a strange dog on his beat, he gets that angry, thinking the other dog's going to sneak some of his grub. And he don't half bite."

Max frisked about merrily and got under the lieutenant's feet, entangling his leash in the officer's sword and altogether displaying extreme delight at being taken for a walk.

They went out into the street and Lieutenant Lukash made for the Prikopy. He had an appointment with a lady at the corner of Panská Street. He was engrossed in official thoughts. What was he to lecture about to the volunteer officers the next day? How is the elevation of a given hill determined? Why is the elevation always measured

above the sea level? How can the simple elevation of a hill from its base be determined from the elevation above the sea level? Confound it, why on earth did the War Office include such rot in its syllabus? That's all very well for the artillery. Besides, there are the general staff maps. If the enemy is on Hill 312, there's no point in wondering why the elevation of the hill is measured above the sea level or in calculating how high it is. You just look at the map, and there you are.

He was disturbed from these reflections by a stern "Halt!" just as he was approaching Panská Street. At the same instant the dog tried to scuttle away from him, lead and all, and gleefully barking, it hurled itself upon the man who had shouted "Halt!"

The lieutenant found himself face to face with Colonel Kraus von Zillergut. He saluted and apologized to the colonel for not having noticed him earlier.

"An officer of lower rank, sir," thundered Colonel Kraus, "must always salute officers of higher rank. That is a regulation which, I believe, is still in force. And there is another thing. Since when have officers been in the habit of promenading in the streets with stolen dogs? Yes, with stolen dogs, I said. A dog which belongs to someone else is a stolen dog."

"This dog, sir—" began Lieutenant Lukash.

"Belongs to me, sir," said the colonel, interrupting him curtly. "That's my dog Fox."

And Fox alias Max remembered his old master, and completely repudiated his new one. He left Lieutenant Lukash in the lurch and began to jump up at the colonel with every appearance of delight.

"To walk about with stolen dogs, sir, is incompatible with an officer's honor. You didn't know? An officer cannot purchase a dog unless he has convinced himself that he can do so without fear of any

untoward consequences." Colonel Kraus continued to bellow as he stroked Max, who now basely began to snarl at the lieutenant and to show his teeth, as if saying to the colonel, "Give it him hot!"

"Would you consider it right, sir," continued the colonel, "to ride on a stolen horse? Didn't you read my advertisement in *Bohemia* and the *Prager Tageblatt* about the loss of my Pomeranian? You didn't read the advertisement that your superior officer put into the papers?"

The colonel banged the fist of one hand into the palm of the other.

"Upon my word, what are these young officers coming to? Where's their sense of discipline? A colonel puts advertisements in the paper and they don't read them."

"By Jove, wouldn't I like to land him a couple across the jaw, the silly old buffer!" thought Lieutenant Lukash to himself as he looked at the colonel's whiskers, which reminded him of an orangutan.

"Just step this way a moment," said the colonel. So they walked along together, engaged in a highly pleasant conversation.

"When you get to the front, you won't be able to get up to tricks of that sort. I've no doubt it's very nice to lounge about at the base and go for walks with stolen dogs. Oh yes! With a dog belonging to your superior officer. At a time when we are losing hundreds of officers every day on the battlefields. And catch them reading advertisements. Not they! Why, damn it all, I might go on advertising for a hundred years that I've lost a dog. Two hundred years, three hundred years!"

The old colonel blew his nose noisily, which in his case was always a sign of great indignation, and said, "You can continue your walk."

Whereupon he turned on his heel and departed, savagely slashing his riding whip across the ends of his greatcoat.

Lieutenant Lukash crossed the road, and there again he heard that yell of "Halt!" The colonel had just stopped an unfortunate infantry reservist who was thinking of his mother and had not noticed him.

With his own hands the colonel conducted him into barracks for punishment, calling him a blithering jackass.

"What am I to do with that fellow Schweik?" thought the lieutenant. "I'll bash his jaw in, but that's not enough. Why, if I was to slice him into strips, it would be too good for a skunk like him."

And disregarding his appointment with the lady, he wrathfully made his way home.

"I'll murder that blighter, that I will," he said to himself, as he got into a tram.

Corey Ford

1902-1969

EVERY DOG SHOULD OWN A MAN

Every dog should have a man of his own. There is nothing like a well-behaved person around the house to spread the dog's blanket for him, or bring him his supper when he comes home man-tired at night.

For example, I happen to belong to an English setter who acquired me when he was about six months old and has been training me quite successfully ever since. He has taught me to shake hands with him and fetch his ball. I've learned not to tug at the leash when he takes me for a walk. I am completely housebroken, and I make him a devoted companion.

The first problem a dog faces is to pick out the right man—a gay and affectionate disposition is more important than an expensive pedigree. I do not happen to be registered but my setter is just as fond of me as though I came from a long line of blue bloods. Also, since a dog is judged by the man he leads, it is a good idea to walk the man up and down a couple of times to make sure his action is free and he has springy hindquarters.

The next question is whether the dog and man should share the house together. Some dogs prefer a kennel because it is more sanitary, but my setter decided at the start that he'd move right in the house with me. I can get into any of the chairs I want except the big overstuffed chair in the living room, which is his.

Training a man takes time. Some men are a little slow to respond, but a dog who makes allowances and tries to put himself in the man's place will be rewarded with a loyal pal. Men are apt to be high-strung and sensitive, and a dog who loses his temper will only break the man's spirit.

Punishment should be meted out sparingly—more can be accomplished by a reproachful look than by flying off the handle. My setter has never raised a paw to me, but he has cured me almost entirely of the habit of running away. When he sees me start to pack my suitcase he just lies down on the floor with his chin on his forepaws and gazes at me sadly. Usually I wind up by canceling my train reservations.

The first thing to teach a man is to stay at heel. For this lesson the dog should hook one end of a leash to his collar and loop the other end around the man's wrist so he cannot get away. Start down the street slowly, pausing at each telephone pole

until the man realizes that he's under control. He may tug and yank at first, but this can be discouraged by slipping deftly between his legs and winding the leash around his ankles. If the man tries to run ahead, brace all four feet and halt suddenly, thus jerking him flat on his back. After a few such experiences the man will follow his dog with docility. Remember, however, that all such efforts at discipline must be treated as sport, and after a man has sprawled on the sidewalk the dog should lick his face to show him it was all in fun.

Every man should learn to retrieve a rubber ball. The way my setter taught me this trick was simple. He would lie in the center of the floor while I carried the ball to the far side of the room and rolled it toward him, uttering the word "Fetch!" He would watch the ball carefully as it rolled past him and under the sofa. I would then get the ball from under the sofa and roll it past him again, giving the same command, "Fetch!"

This lesson would be repeated until the setter was asleep. After I got so I would retrieve the ball every time I said "Fetch!" my dog substituted other articles for me to pick up, such as an old marrow bone or a piece of paper he found in the wastebasket.

The matter of physical conditioning is important. A man whose carriage is faulty, and who slouches and droops his tail, is a reflection on the dog who owns him. The best way to keep him in shape is to work him constantly and never give him a chance to relax. Racing him up and down the street at the end of a leash is a great conditioner. If he attempts to slump into an easy chair when he gets back, the dog should leap into it ahead of him and force him to sit in a straight-backed chair to improve his posture. And be sure to get him up several times a night to go out for a walk, especially if it is raining.

Equally important is diet. Certain liquids such as beer have a tendency to bloat a man, and a dog should teach him restraint by jumping up at him and spilling his drink, or tactfully knocking the glass off the table with a sweep of his tail.

Not every dog who tries to bring up a man is as successful as my setter. The answer lies in understanding. The dog must be patient and not work himself into a tantrum if his man can't learn to chase rabbits or wriggle under fences as well as the dog does. After all, as my setter says, it's hard to teach an old man new tricks.

No one appreciates the very special genius of your conversation as a dog does.

Christopher Morley

Is Your Dog Popular?

AMERICAN
KENNEL CLUB
REGISTRATIONS

		1977	1976
1	Poodles	112,300	126,799
2	Doberman Pinschers	79,254	73,615
3	German Shepherd Dogs	67,072	74,723
4	Cocker Spaniels	52,955	46,862
5	Irish Setters	43,367	54,917
6	Labrador Retrievers	41,275	39,929
7	Beagles	40,850	44,156
8	Dachshunds	35,087	38,927
9	Miniature Schnauzers	35,072	36,816
10	Golden Retrievers	30,263	27,612
11	Shetland Sheepdogs	24,464	23,950
12	Collies	23,386	25,161
13	Lhasa Apsos	22,354	21,145
14	Yorkshire Terriers	21,573	20,392
15	Siberian Huskies	20,196	20,598
16	Pekingese	19,891	20,400
17	Brittany Spaniels	19,267	20,222
18	English Springer Spaniels	18,579	16,842
19	Great Danes	17,892	19,869
20	Pomeranians	15,943	15,241
21	Chihuahuas	15,841	16,478
22	Old English Sheepdogs	14,403	15,364
23	Basset Hounds	14,368	14,997
24	Shih Tzu	14,189	12,562
25	St. Bernards	13,186	17,537
26	German Shorthaired Pointers	13,093	14,269
27	Boxers	12,951	13,057
28	Boston Terriers	10,753	10,806
29	Samoyeds	9,640	10,147
30	Afghan Hounds	9,416	10,045
31	Alaskan Malamutes	8,371	8,324

32	Chow Chows...........	7,649	6,211
33	Norwegian Elkhounds...	7,280	8,037
34	Scottish Terriers........	7,073	7,202
35	Airdale Terriers........	6,745	6,835
36	Dalmatians...........	6,694	7,241
37	Bulldogs.............	6,549	6,554
38	Cairn Terriers........	6,359	6,432
39	West Highland White Terriers............	6,332	6,072
40	Maltese.............	6,197	6,183
41	Pugs...............	6,066	6,660
42	Keeshonden...........	6,040	5,871
43	Weimaraners..........	5,519	6,243
44	Fox Terriers..........	4,254	4,673
45	Chesapeake Bay Retrievers	2,906	2,650
46	Silky Terriers.........	2,728	2,829
47	Welsh Corgis(Pembroke).	2,179	2,061
48	Newfoundlands........	2,069	2,113
49	Rottweillers..........	1,878	1,406
50	Vizslas.............	1,877	1,867
51	Basenjis............	1,702	1,674
52	Bichons Frises........	1,619	1,512
53	English Setters.......	1,579	1,756
54	Bloodhounds..........	1,578	1,446
55	Borzois.............	1,535	1,658
56	Irish Wolfhounds.......	1,383	1,409
57	Great Pyrenees........	1,364	1,529
58	Akitas.............	1,332	1,213
59	Gordon Setters.......	1,329	1,383
60	Miniature Pinschers.....	1,316	1,126
61	Schipperkes...........	1,272	1,260
62	Bouviers Des Flandres...	1,204	1,053
63	Whippets............	1,146	1,050
64	Bull Terriers..........	1,057	929
65	English Cocker Spaniels..	1,024	942
66	German Wirehaired Pointers............	969	1,021
67	Mastiffs.............	936	810
68	American Staffordshire Terriers............	904	732
69	Rhodesian Ridgeback....	872	846
70	Australian Terriers......	847	939
71	Bullmastiffs..........	821	676
72	Welsh Terriers........	782	888
73	Standard Schnauzers....	772	785
74	Salukis.............	743	737
75	Soft-Coated Wheaten Terriers............	650	539
76	Kerry Blue Terriers.....	621	661
77	Papillons............	547	490
78	Belgian Sheepdogs......	534	552
79	Giant Schnauzers.......	499	565
80	Pulik..............	480	609
81	Italian Greyhounds.....	478	506
82	Bearded Collies........	446	998

83	Pointers.............	429	439
84	Manchester Terriers.....	406	536
85	Belgian Tervuren.......	397	430
86	Irish Terriers.........	385	273
87	Bedlington Terriers.....	380	370
88	Japanese Chin........	368	356
89	Welsh Corgis (Cardigan)..	364	356
90	Black and Tan Coonhounds	326	357
91	Bernese Mountain Dogs..	324	292
92	American Water Spaniels.	323	302
93	Norwich Terriers.......	295	278
94	Tibetan Terriers.......	275	242
95	Staffordshire Bull Terriers	256	291
96	Briards.............	254	216
97	Dandie Dinmont Terriers.	226	235
98	Skye Terriers.........	216	226
99	French Bulldogs........	195	208
100	Greyhounds...........	188	148
101	Brussels Griffons.......	178	219
102	Lakeland Terriers.......	176	171
103	Kuvaszok............	170	158
104	Flat-Coated Retrievers ...	156	132
105	Sealyham Terriers......	154	98
106	Irish Water Spaniels.....	142	89
107	Welsh Springer Spaniels..	137	108
108	Scottish Deerhounds....	124	158
109	Wirehaired Pointing Griffons.............	117	137
110	Border Terriers........	110	104
111	Komondorok..........	99	99
112	Foxhounds (American) ..	84	69
113	Affenpinschers.........	77	63
114	Clumber Spaniels.......	61	55
115	English Toy Spaniels....	58	46
116	Otter Hounds.........	49	52
117	Curly-Coated Retrievers..	45	15
118	Belgian Malinois.......	36	34
119	Field Spaniels.........	31	42
120	Harriers.............	15	25
121	Sussex Spaniels........	7	14
122	Foxhounds (English)....	4	9

	1,013,650	1,048,648

Anatole France

1844-1924

THE COMING OF RIQUET

Seated at his table one morning in front of the window, against which the leaves of the plane tree quivered, M. Bergeret, who was trying to discover how the ships of Aeneas had been changed into nymphs, heard a tap at the door, and forthwith his servant entered, carrying in front of her, opossum-like, a tiny creature whose black head peeped out from the folds of her apron, which she had turned up to form a pocket. With a look of anxiety and hope upon her face she remained motionless for a moment, then she placed the little thing upon the carpet at her master's feet.

"What's that?" asked M. Bergeret.

It was a little dog of doubtful breed, having something of the terrier in him, and a well-set head, a short, smooth coat of a dark tan color, and a tiny little stump of a tail. His body retained its puppy-like softness, and he went sniffling at the carpet.

"Angélique," said M. Bergeret, "take this animal back to its owner."

"It has no owner, Monsieur."

M. Bergeret looked silently at the little creature, who had come to examine his slippers, and was giving little sniffs of approval. M. Bergeret was a philologist, which perhaps explains why at this juncture he asked a vain question.

"What is he called?"

"Monsieur," replied Angélique, "he has no name."

M. Bergeret seemed put out at this answer: he looked at the dog sadly, with a disheartened air.

Then the little animal placed its two front paws on M. Bergeret's slipper, and, holding it thus, began innocently to nibble at it. With a sudden access of compassion M. Bergeret took the tiny nameless creature upon his knee. The dog looked at him intently, and M. Bergeret was pleased at his confiding expression.

"What beautiful eyes!" he cried.

The dog's eyes were indeed beautiful, the pupils of a golden-flecked chestnut set in warm white. And his gaze spoke of simple, mysterious thoughts, common alike to the thoughtful beasts and simple men of the earth.

Tired, perhaps, with the intellectual effort he had made for the purpose of entering into communication with a human being, he closed his beautiful eyes, and, yawning widely, revealed his pink mouth, his curled-up tongue, and his array of dazzling teeth.

M. Bergeret put his hand into the dog's mouth, and allowed him to lick it, at which old Angélique gave a smile of relief.

"A more affectionate little creature doesn't breathe," she said.

"The dog," said M. Bergeret, "is a religious animal. In his savage state he worships the moon and the lights that float upon the waters. These are his gods, to whom he appeals at night with long-drawn howls. In the domesticated state he seeks by his caresses to conciliate those powerful genii who dispense the good things of this world—to wit, men. He worships and honors men by the accomplishment of the rites passed down to him by his ancestors: he licks their hands, jumps against their legs, and when they show signs of anger towards him he approaches them crawling on his belly as a sign of humility, to appease their wrath."

"All dogs are not the friends of man," remarked Angélique. "Some of them bite the hand that feeds them."

"Those are the ungodly, blasphemous dogs," returned M. Bergeret, "insensate creatures like Ajax, the son of Telamon, who wounded the hand of the golden Aphrodite. These sacrilegious creatures die a dreadful death, or lead wandering and miserable lives. They are not to be confounded with those dogs who, espousing the quarrel of their own particular god, wage war upon his enemy, the neighboring god. They are heroes. Such, for example, is the dog of Lafolie, the butcher who fixed his sharp teeth into the leg of the tramp Pied-d'Alouette. For it is a fact that dogs fight among themselves like men, and Turk, with his snub nose, serves his god Lafolie against the robber gods, in the same way that Israel helped Jehovah to destroy Chamos and Moloch."

The puppy, however, having decided that M. Bergeret's remarks were the reverse of interesting, curled up his feet and stretched out his head, ready to go to sleep upon the knees that harbored him.

"Where did you find him?" asked M. Bergeret.

"Well, Monsieur, it was Dellion's *chef* gave him to me."

"With the result," continued M. Bergeret, "that we now have this soul to care for."

"What soul?" asked Angélique.

"This canine soul. An animal is, properly speaking, a soul; I do not say an immortal soul. And yet, when I come to consider the positions this poor little beast and I myself occupy in the scheme of things, I recognize in both exactly the same right to immortality."

After considerable hesitation, old Angélique, with a painful effort that made her upper lip curl up and reveal her two remaining teeth, said:

"If Monsieur does not want a dog, I will return him to M. Dellion's *chef;* but you may safely keep him, I assure you. You won't see or hear him."

She had hardly finished her sentence when the puppy, hearing a heavy van rolling down the street, sat bolt upright on M. Bergeret's knees, and began to bark both loud and long, so that the windowpanes resounded with the noise.

M. Bergeret smiled.

"He's a watch-dog," said Angélique, by way of excuse. "They are by far the most faithful."

"Have you given him anything to eat?" asked M. Bergeret.

"Of course," returned Angélique.

"What does he eat?"

"Monsieur must be aware that dogs eat bread and meat."

Somewhat piqued, M. Bergeret retorted that in her eagerness she might very likely have taken him away from his mother before he was old enough to leave her, upon which he was lifted up again and re-examined, only to make sure of the fact that he was at least six months old.

M. Bergeret put him down on the carpet, and regarded him with interest.

"Isn't he pretty?" said the servant.

"No, he is not pretty," replied M. Bergeret. "But he is engaging, and has beautiful eyes. That is what people used to say about me," added the professor, "when I was three times as old, and not half as intelligent. Since then I have no doubt acquired an outlook upon the universe, which he will never attain. But, in comparison with the Absolute, I may say that my knowledge equals his in the smallness of its extent. Like his, it is a geometrical point in the infinite." Then, addressing the little creature who was sniffing the waste-paper basket, he went on: "Smell it out, sniff it well, take from the outside world all the knowledge that can reach your simple brain through the medium of that black truffle-like nose of yours. And what though I at the same time observe, and compare, and study? We shall never know, neither the one nor the other of us, why we have been put into this world, and what we are doing in it. What are we here for, eh?"

As he had spoken rather loudly, the puppy looked at him anxiously, and M. Bergeret, returning to the thought which had first filled his mind, said to the servant:

"We must give him a name."

With her hands folded in front of her she replied laughingly that would not be a difficult matter.

Upon which M. Bergeret made the private reflection that to the simple all things are simple, but that clear-sighted souls, who look upon things from many and divers aspects, invisible to the vulgar mind, experience the greatest difficulty in coming to a decision about even the most trivial matters. And he cudgelled his brains, trying to hit upon a name for the little living thing that was busily engaged in nibbling the fringe of the carpet.

"All the names of dogs," thought he, "preserved in the ancient treatises of the huntsmen of old, such as Fouilloux, and in the verses of our sylvan poets such as La Fontaine—Finaud, Miraut, Briffaut, Ravaud, and such-like names, are given to sporting dogs, who are the aristocracy of the kennel, the chivalry of the canine race. The dog of Ulysses was called Argos, and he was a hunter too, so Homer tells us. 'In his youth he hunted the little hares of Ithaca, but now he was old and hunted no more.' What we require is something quite different. The names given by old maids to their lapdogs would be more suitable, were they not usually pretentious and absurd. Azor, for instance, is ridiculous!"

So M. Bergeret ruminated, calling to memory many a dog name, without being able to decide, however, on one that pleased him. He would have liked to invet a name, but lacked the imagination.

"What day is it?" he asked at last.

"The ninth," replied Angélique. "Thursday, the ninth."

"Well, then!" said M. Bergeret, "can't we call the dog Thursday, like Robinson Crusoe who called his man Friday, for the same reason?"

"As Monsieur pleases," said Angélique. "But it isn't very pretty."

"Very well," said M. Bergeret, "find a name for the creature yourself, for, after all, you brought him here."

"Oh, no," said the servant. "I couldn't find a name for him; I'm not clever enough. When I saw him lying on the straw in the kitchen, I called him Riquet, and he came up and played about under my skirts."

"You called him Riquet, did you?" cried M. Bergeret. "Why didn't you say so before? Riquet he is and Riquet he shall remain; that's settled. Now be off with you, and take Riquet with you. I want to work."

"Monsieur," returned Angélique, "I am going to leave the puppy with you; I will come for him when I get back from market."

"You could quite well take him to market with you," retorted M. Bergeret.

"Monsieur, I am going to church as well."

It was quite true that she really was going to church at Saint-Exupère, to ask for a Mass to be said for the repose of her husband's soul. She did that regularly once a year, not that she had even been informed of the decease of Borniche, who had never communicated with her since his desertion, but it was a settled thing in the good woman's mind that Borniche was dead. She had therefore no fear of his coming to rob her of the little she had, and did her best to fix things up to his advantage in the other world, so long as he left her in peace in this one.

"Eh!" ejaculated M. Bergeret. "Shut him up in the kitchen or some other convenient place, and do not wor——"

He did not finish his sentence, for Angélique had vanished, purposely pretending not to hear, that she might leave Riquet with his master. She wanted them to grow used to one another, and she also wanted to give poor, friendless M. Bergeret a companion. Having closed the door behind her, she went along the corridor and down the steps.

M. Bergeret set to work again and plunged head foremost into his *Virgilius nauticus*. He loved the work; it rested his thoughts, and became a kind of game that suited him, for he played it all by himself. On the table beside him were several boxes filled with pegs, which he fixed into little squares of cardboard to represent the fleet of Aeneas. Now

while he was thus occupied he felt something like tiny fists tapping at his legs. Riquet, whom he had quite forgotten, was standing on his hind legs patting his master's knees, and wagging his little stump of a tail. When he tired of this, he let his paws slide down the trouser leg, then got up and began his coaxing over again. And M. Bergeret, turning away from the printed lore before him, saw two brown eyes gazing up at him lovingly.

"What gives a human beauty to the gaze of this dog," he thought, "is probably that it varies unceasingly, being by turns bright and vivacious, or serious and sorrowful; because through these eyes his little dumb soul finds expression for thought that lacks nothing in depth nor sequence. My father was very fond of cats, and, consequently, I liked them too. He used to declare that cats are the wise man's best companions, for they respect his studious hours. Bajazet, his Persian cat, would sit at night for hours at a stretch, motionless and majestic, perched on a corner of his table. I still remember the agate eyes of Bajazet, but those jewel-like orbs concealed all thought, that owl-like stare was cold, and hard, and wicked. How much do I prefer the melting gaze of the dog!"

Riquet, however, was agitating his paws in frantic fashion, and M. Bergeret, who was anxious to return to his philological amusements, said kindly, but shortly:

"Lie down, Riquet!"

Upon which Riquet went and thrust his nose against the door through which Angélique had passed out. And there he remained, uttering from time to time plaintive, meek little cries. After a while he began to scratch, making a gentle rasping noise on the polished floor with his nails. Then the whining began again followed by more scratching. Disturbed by these sounds, M. Bergeret sternly bade him keep still.

Riquet peered at him sorrowfully with his brown eyes, then, sitting down, he looked at M. Bergeret again, rose, returned to the door, sniffed underneath it, and wailed afresh.

"Do you want to go out?" asked M. Bergeret.

Putting down his pen, he went to the door, which he held a few inches open. After making sure that he was running no risk of hurting himself on the way out, Riquet slipped through the doorway and marched off with a composure that was scarcely polite. On returning to his table, M. Bergeret, sensitive man that he was, pondered over the dog's action. He said to himself:

"I was on the point of reproaching the animal for going without saying either good-bye or thank you, and expecting him to apologize for leaving me.

It was the beautiful human expression of his eyes that made me so foolish. I was beginning to look upon him as one of my own kind."

After making this reflection M. Bergeret applied himself anew to the metamorphosis of the ships of Aeneas, a legend both pretty and popular, but perhaps a trifle too simple in itself for expression in such noble language. M. Bergeret, however, saw nothing incongruous in it. He knew that the nursery tales have furnished material for nearly all epics, and that Virgl had carefully collected together in his poem the riddles, the puns, the uncouth stories, and the puerile imaginings of his forefathers; that Homer, his master and the master of all the bards, had done little more than tell over again what the good wives of Ionia and the fishermen of the islands had been narrating for more than a thousand years before him. Besides, for the time being, this was the least of his worries; he had another far more important preoccupation. An expression, met with in the course of the charming story of the metamorphosis, did not appear sufficiently plain to him. That was what was worrying him.

"Bergeret, my friend," he said to himself, "this is where you must open your eyes and show your sense. Remember that Virgil always expresses himself with extreme precision when writing on the technique of the arts; remember that he went yachting at Baïae, that he was an expert in naval constuction, and that therefore his language, in this passage, must have a precise and definite signification."

And M. Bergeret carefully consulted a great number of texts, in order to throw a light upon the word which he could not understand, and which he had to explain. He was almost on the point of grasping the solution, or, at any rate, he had caught a glimpse of it, when he heard a noise like the rattling of chains at his door, a noise which, although not alarming, struck him as curious. The disturbance was presently accompanied by a shrill whining, and M. Bergeret, interrupted in his philological investigations, immediately concluded that these importunate wails must emanate from Riquet.

As a matter of fact, after having looked vainly all over the house for Angélique, Riquet had been seized with a desire to see M. Bergeret again. Solitude was as painful to him as human society was dear. In order to put an end to the noise, and also because he had a secret desire to see Riquet again, M. Bergeret got up from his arm-chair and opened the door, and Riquet re-entered the study with the same coolness with which he had quitted it, but as soon as he saw the door close behind him he assumed a melancholy expression, and began to wander up and down the room like a soul in torment.

He had a sudden way of appearing to find something of interest beneath the chairs and tables, and would sniff long and noisily; then he would walk aimlessly about or sit down in a corner with an air of great humility, like the beggars who are to be seen in church porches. Finally he began to bark at a cast of Hermes which stood upon the mantelshelf, whereupon M. Bergeret addressed him in words full of just reproach.

"Riquet! such vain agitation, such sniffing and barking were better suited to a stable than to the study of a professor, and they lead one to suppose that your ancestors lived with those horses whose straw litters they shared. I do not reproach you with that. It is only natural you should have inherited their habits, manners, and tendencies as well as their close-cropped coat, their sausage-like body, and their long, thin nose. I do not speak of your beautiful eyes, for there are few men, few dogs even, who can open such beauties to the light of day. But, leaving all that aside, you are a mongrel, my friend, a mongrel from your short, bandy legs to your head. Again I am far from despising you for that. What I want you to understand is that if you desire to live with me, you will have to drop your mongrel manners and behave like a *scholar*, in other words, to remain silent and quiet, to respect work, after the manner of Bajazet, who of a night would sit for hours without stirring, and watch my father's pen skimming over the paper. He was a silent and tactful creature. How different is your own character, my friend! Since you came into this chamber of study your hoarse voice, your unseemly snufflings and your whines, that sound like steam whistles, have constantly confused my thoughts and interrupted by reflections. And now you have made me lose the drift of an important passage in Servius, referring to the constuction of one of the ships of Aeneas. Know then, Riquet, my friend, that this is the house of silence and the abode of meditation, and that if you are anxious to stay here you must become literary. Be quiet!"

Thus spoke M. Bergeret. Riquet, who had listened to him with mute astonishment, approached his master, and with suppliant gesture placed a timid paw upon the knee, which he seemed to revere in a fashion that savored of long ago. Then a kind thought struck M. Bergeret. He picked him up by the scruff of his neck, and put him upon the cushions of the ample easy chair in which he was sitting. Turning himself round three times, Riquet lay down, and then remained perfectly still and silent. He was quite happy. M. Bergeret was grateful to him, and as he ran through Servius he occasionally stroked the close-cropped coat, which, without being soft, was smooth and very pleasant to the touch. Riquet fell into a gentle doze, and communicated to his master the generous warmth of his body, the subtle, gentle heat of a living, breathing thing. And from that moment M. Bergeret found more pleasure in his *Virgilius mauticus*.

From floor to ceiling his study was lined with deal shelves bearing books arranged in methodical order. One glance, and all that remains to us of Latin thought was ready to his hand. The Greeks lay halfway up. In a quiet corner, easy to access, were Rabelais, the excellent story-tellers of the *Cent nouvelles nouvelles*, Bonaventure des Périers, Guillaume Bouchet, and all the old French "conteurs," whom M. Bergeret considered better adapted to humanity than writings in the more heroic style, and who were the favorite reading of his leisure. He possessed them in cheap modern editions only, but he had discovered a poor bookbinder in the town who covered his volumes with leaves from a book of anthems, and it gave M. Bergeret the keenest pleasure to see these free-spoken gentlemen thus clad in Requiems and Misereres. This was the sole luxury and the only peculiarity of his austere library. The other books were paper-backed or bound in poor and worn-out bindings. The gentle friendly manner in which they were handled by their owner gave them the look of tools set out in a busy man's workshop. The books of archaeology and art found a resting-place on the highest shelves, not by any means out of contempt, but because they were not so often used.

Now, while M. Bergeret worked at his *Virgilius nauticus* and shared his chair with Riquet, he found, as chance would have it, that it was necessary to consult Ottfried Müller's little *Manual*, which happened to be on one of the topmost shelves.

There was no need of one of those tall ladders on wheels topped by railings and a shelf, to enable him to reach the book; there were ladders of this description in the town library, and they had been used by all the great book-lovers of the eighteenth and nineteenth centuries; indeed, several of the latter had fallen from them, and thus died honorable deaths, in the manner spoken of in the pamphlet entitled: *Des bibliophiles qui moururent en tombant de leur échelle.* No, indeed! M. Bergeret had no need of anything of the sort. A small pair of folding steps would have served his purpose excellently well, and he had once seen some in the shop of Clérambaut, the cabinet-maker, in the Rue de Josde. They folded up, and looked just the thing, with their bevelled uprights each pierced with a trefoil as a grip for the hand. M. Bergeret would have given anything to possess them, but the state of his finances, which were somewhat involved, forced him to abandon the idea. No one knew better than he did that financial ills are not mortal, but, for all that, he had no steps in his study.

In place of such a pair of steps he used an old cane-bottomed chair, the back of which had been broken, leaving only two horns or antennae, which had shown themselves to be more dangerous than useful. So they had been cut to the level of the seat, and the chair had become a stool. There were two reasons why this stool was ill-fitted to the use to which M. Bergeret was wont to put it. In the first place the woven-cane seat had grown slack with long use, and now contained a large hollow, making one's foothold precarious. In the second place the stool was too low, and it was hardly possible when standing upon it to reach the books on the highest shelf, even with the finger-tips. What generally happened was that in the endeavor to grasp one book, several others fell out; and it depended upon their being bound or paper-covered whether they lay with broken corners, or sprawled with leaves spread like a fan or a concertina.

Now, with the intention of getting down the *Manual* of Ottfried Müller, M. Bergeret quitted the chair he was sharing with Riquet, who, rolled into a ball with his head tight pressed to his body, lay in warm comfort, opening one voluptuous eye, which he re-closed as quickly. Then M. Bergeret drew the stool from the dark corner where it was hidden and placed it where it was required, hoisted himself upon it, and managed, by making his arm as long as possible, and straining upon tiptoe, to touch, first with one, then with two fingers, the back of a book which he judged to be the one he was needing. As for the thumb, it remained below the shelf and rendered no assistance whatever. M. Bergeret, who found it therefore exceedingly difficult to draw out the book, made the reflection that the reason why the hand is a precious implement is on account of the position of the thumb, and that no being could rise to be an artist who had four feet and no hands.

"It is to the hand," he reflected, "that men owe their power of becoming engineers, painters, writers, and manipulators of all kinds of things. If they had no thumb as well as their other fingers, they would be as incapable as I am at this moment, and they could never have changed the face of the earth as they have done. Beyond a doubt it is the shape of the hand that has assured to man the conquest of the world."

Then, almost simultaneously, M. Bergeret remembered that monkeys, who posses four hands, have not, for all that, created the arts, nor disposed that earth to their use, and he erased from his mind the theory upon which he had just embarked. However, he did the best he could with his four fingers. It must be known that Ottfried Müller's *Manual* is composed of three volumes and an atlas. M. Bergeret wanted volume one. He pulled out first the second volume, then the atlas, then volume three, and finally the book that he required. At last he held it in his hands. All that now remained for him to do

was to descend, and this he was about to do when the cane seat gave way beneath his foot, which passed through it. He lost his balance and fell to the ground, not as heavily as might have been feared, for he broke his fall by grasping at one of the uprights of the bookshelf.

He was on the ground, however, full of astonishment, and wearing on one leg the broken chair; his whole body was permeated and as though constricted by a pain that spread all over it, and that presently settled itself more particularly in the region of the left elbow and hip upon which he had fallen. But, as his anatomy was not seriously damaged, he gathered his wits together; he had got so far as to realize that he must draw his right leg out of the stool in which it had so unfortunately become entangled, and that he must be careful to raise himself upon on his right side, which was unhurt. He was even trying to put this into execution when he felt a warm breath upon his cheek, and turning his eyes, which fright and pain had for the moment fixed, he saw close to his cheek Riquet's little face.

At the sound of the fall Riquet had jumped down from the chair and run to his unfortunate master; he was now standing near him in a state of great excitement; then he commenced to run round him. First he came near out of sympathy, then he retreated out of fear of some mysterious danger. He understood perfectly well that a misfortune had taken place, but he was neither thoughtful nor clever enough to discover what it was; hence his anxiety. His fidelity drew him to his suffering friend, and his prudence stopped him on the very brink of the fatal spot. Encouraged at length by the calm and silence which eventually reigned, he licked M. Bergeret's neck and looked at him with eyes of fear and of love. The fallen master smiled, and the dog licked the end of his nose. It was a great comfort to M. Bergeret, who freed his right leg, stood erect, and limped good-humoredly back to his chair.

Riquet was there before him. All that could be seen of his eyes was a gleam between the narrow slit of the half-closed lids. He seemed to have forgotten all about the adventure that a moment before had so stirred them both. The little creature lived in the present, with no thought of time that had run its course; not that he was wanting in memory, inasmuch as he could remember, not his own past alone, but the faraway past of his ancestors, and his little head was a rich storehouse of useful knowledge; but he took no pleasure in remembrance, and memory was not for him, as it was for M. Bergeret, a divine muse.

Gently stroking the short, smooth coat of his companion, M. Bergeret addressed him in the following affectionate terms:

"Dog! at the price of the repose which is dear to your heart, you came to me when I was dismayed and brought low. You did not laugh, as any young person of my own species would have done. It is true that however joyous or terrible nature may appear to you at times, she never inspires you with a sense of the ridiculous. And it is for that very reason, because of your innocent gravity, that you are the surest friend a man can have. In the first instance I inspired confidence and admiration in you, and now you show me pity.

"Dog! when we first met on the highway of life, we came from the two poles of creation; we belong to different species. I refer to this with no desire to take advantage of it, but rather with a strong sense of universal brotherhood. We have hardly been acquainted two hours, and my hand has never yet fed you. What can be the meaning of the obscure love for me that has sprung up in your little heart? The sympathy you bestow on me is a charming mystery, and I accept it. Sleep, friend, in the place that you have chosen!"

Having thus spoken, M. Bergeret turned over the leaves of Ottfried Müller's *Manual*, which with marvelous instinct he had kept in his hand both during and after his fall. He turned over the pages, and could not find what he sought.

Every moment, however, seemed to increase the pain he was feeling.

"I believe," he thought, "that the whole of my left side is bruised and my hip swollen. I have a suspicion that my right leg is grazed all over and my left elbow aches and burns, but shall I cavil at pain that has led me to the discovery of a friend?"

His reflections were running thus when old Angélique, breathless and perspiring, entered the study. She first opened the door, and then she knocked, for she never permitted herself to enter without knocking. If she had not done so before she opened the door, she did it after, for she had good manners, and knew what was expected of her. She went in therefore, knocked, and said:

"Monsieur, I have come to relieve you of the dog."

M. Bergeret heard these words with decided annoyance. He had not as yet inquired into his claims to Riquet, and now realized that he had none. The thought that Madame Borniche might take the animal away from his filled him with sadness, yet, after all, Riquet did belong to her. Affecting indifference, he replied:

"He's asleep; let him sleep!"

"Where is he? I don't see him," remarked old Angélique.

"Here he is," answered M. Bergeret. "In my chair."

With her two hands clasped over her portly figure, old Angélique smiled, and, in a tone of gentle mockery, ventured:

"I wonder what pleasure the creature can find in sleeping there behind Monsieur!"

"That," retorted M. Bergeret, "is his business."

Then, as he was of inquiring mind, he immediately sought of Riquet his reasons for the selection of his resting-place, and lighting on them, replied with his accustomed candor:

"I keep him warm, and my presence affords a sence of security; my comrade is a chilly and homely little animal." Then he added: "Do you know, Angélique? I will go out presently and buy him a collar."

Dachshunds are ideal dogs for small children, as they are already stretched and pulled to such a length that the child cannot do much harm one way or the other.   *Robert Benchley*

When a doting person gets down on all fours and plays with his dog's rubber mouse, it only confuses the puppy and gives him a sense of insecurity. He gets the impression that the world is unstable, and wonders whether he is supposed to walk on his hind legs and learn to smoke cigars.   *Corey Ford*

Anecdotes

Nineteenth Century

HISTORY OF
ANIMALS

A grocer in Edinburgh had a Dog, which for some time amused and astonished the people in the neighborhood. A man who went through the streets ringing a bell and selling penny pies, happened one day to treat this Dog with a pie. The next time he heard the pieman's bell, the Dog ran to him with impetuosity, seized him by the coat, and would not suffer him to pass. The pieman, who understood what the animal wanted, showed him a penny, and pointed to his master, who stood at the street-door and saw what was going on. The Dog immediately supplicated his master by many humble gestures and looks. The master put a penny into the Dog's mouth, which he instantly delivered to the pieman, and received his pie; and this traffic between the pieman and the grocer's Dog, continued to be daily practised for many months.

At a convent in France, twenty paupers were served with a dinner at a certain hour every day. A Dog belonging to the convent did not fail to be present at this regale, to receive the scraps which were now and then thrown to him. The guests, however, were poor and hungry, and of course not very wasteful; so that their pensioner did little more than scent the feast of which he would fain have partaken. The portions were served by a person, at the ringing of a bell, and delivered out by means of what in religious houses is called a *tour;* a machine like the section of a cask, that, by turning round upon a pivot, exhibits whatever is placed on the concave side, without discovering the person who moves it. One day this Dog, which had only received a few scraps, waited till the paupers were all gone, took the rope in his mouth and rang the bell. His stratagem succeeded. He repeated it the next day with the same good fortune. At length the cook, finding that twenty-one portions were given out instead of twenty, was determined to discover the trick; in doing which he had no great difficulty, for, lying in wait, and noticing the paupers as they came for their different portions, and that there was no intruder except the Dog, he began to suspect the truth; which he was confirmed in when he saw the animal continue with great deliberation till the visitors were all gone, and then pull the bell. The matter was related to the community; and to reward him for his ingenuity, the Dog was permitted to ring the bell every day for his dinner, on which a mess of broken victuals was always afterwards served out to him.

Mr. C. Hughes, a country comedian, had a wig which generally hung on a peg in one of his rooms. He one day lent the wig to a brother player, and some time afterwards called on him. Mr. Hughes had his Dog with him, and the man happened to have the borrowed wig on his head. Mr. Hughes stayed a little while with his friend; but, when he left him, the Dog remained behind. For some time he stood, looking full in the man's face; then, making a sudden spring, he leaped on his shoulders, seized the wig, and ran off with it as fast as he could; and when he reached home, he endeavored, by jumping, to hang it up in its usual place. The same Dog was one afternoon passing through a field near Dartmouth, where a washer-woman had hung out her linen to dry. He stopped and surveyed one particular shirt with attention; then seizing it, he dragged it away through the dirt to his master, whose shirt it proved to be.

In the year 1791, a person went to a house in Deptford, to take lodgings, under pretence that he had just arrived from the West Indies; and, after having agreed on the terms, said he should send his trunk that night, and come himself the next day. About nine o'clock in the evening, the trunk was brought by two porters and was carried into a bedroom. Just as the family were going to bed, their little house-dog, deserting his usual station in the shop, placed himself close to the chamber-door, where the chest was deposited, and kept up an incessant barking. The moment the door was opened, the Dog flew to the chest, against which it scratched and barked with redoubled fury. They attempted to get the Dog out of the room, but in vain. Calling in some neighbors, and making them eye-witnesses of the circumstance, they began to move the trunk about; when they quickly discovered that it contained something that was alive. Suspicion becoming very strong, they were induced to force it open; when, to their utter astonishment, they found in it their new lodger, who had thus been conveyed into the house with the intention of robbing it.

Anton Chekhov

1860-1904

A MARRIAGE PROPOSAL

Scene VI

(NATÁLIA *and* LÓMOV)

LÓMOV (*entering, exhausted*): What horrible palpitations…my foot's gone numb…there's a jabbing in my side…

NATÁLIA: My apologies, Iván Vassílievich, we got so worked up….I do recall now that, the Ox Meadows are actually *your* property.

LÓMOV: My heart's palpitating….The Meadows *are* mine….There are stars bursting in both my eyes.

(*They sit down.*)

NATÁLIA: We were wrong.

LÓMOV: It's the principle of the thing….I don't care about the land, it's the principle of the thing—

NATÁLIA: Exactly, the principle….Let's talk about something else.

LÓMOV: Particularly since I have proof. My aunt's grandmother let your paternal great-grandfather's peasants—

NATÁLIA: All right, all right….(*Aside.*) I don't know how to go about it….(*To* LÓMOV) Will you start hunting soon?

LÓMOV: Yes, for grouse, Natália Stepánovna. I think I shall begin after the harvest. Oh, have you heard what bad luck I had? My hound Guess—you know the one—he's gone lame.

NATÁLIA: What a pity! How did it happen?

LÓMOV: I don't know. He must have twisted his leg, or else some other dog bit him….(*Sighs.*) My very best hound, not to mention the money! Why, I paid Mirónov a hundred and twenty-five rubles for him.

NATÁLIA: You overpaid him, Ivan Vassilievich.

LÓMOV: I don't think so. It was very little for a wonderful dog.

NATÁLIA: Papa bought his dog Leap for eighty-five rubles and Leap is vastly superior to your Guess.

LÓMOV: Leap superior to Guess? Oh, come now. (*Laughs.*) Leap superior to Guess!

NATÁLIA: Of course he is! I know that Leap is still young, he's not a full-grown hound yet. But for points and action, not even Volchanietsky has a better dog.

LÓMOV: Excuse me, Natália Stepánovna, but you're forgetting that he's pug-jawed, which makes him a poor hunting dog.

NATÁLIA: Pug-jawed? That's news to me.

LÓMOV: I can assure you, his lower jaw is shorter than his upper jaw.

NATÁLIA: Have you measured it?

LÓMOV: Indeed, I have. He'll do for pointing, of course, but when it comes to retrieving, he can hardly hold a cand—

NATÁLIA: First of all, our Leap is a pedigreed greyhound—he's the son of Harness and Chisel, whereas your Guess is so piebald that not even Solomon could figure out his breed....Furthermore, he's as old and ugly as a broken-down nag—

LÓMOV: He may be old, but I wouldn't trade him for five of your Leaps....The very idea! Guess is a real hound, but Leap...Why argue? It's ridiculous. ...Every huntsman's assistant has a dog like your Leap. At twenty-five rubles he'd be overpriced.

NATÁLIA: You seem to be possessed by some demon of contradiction, Iván Vassílievich. First you fancy that the Ox Meadows are yours, then you pretend that Guess is a better hound than Leap. If there's one thing I don't like it's a person who says the opposite of what he thinks. You know perfectly well that Leap is a hundred times better than...than that stupid Guess of yours. Why do you insist on denying it?

LÓMOV: You obviously must think, Natália Stepánovna that I'm either blind or mentally retarded. Can't you see that your Leap has a pug jaw?

NATÁLIA: That's not true.

LÓMOV: A pug jaw.

NATÁLIA: (screaming): That's not true.

LÓMOV: Why are you screaming, Madam?

NATÁLIA: Why are you talking such rubbish? It's exasperating! Your Guess is just about ready to be put out of his misery, and you compare him to Leap.

LÓMOV: Excuse me, but I can't keep on arguing like this. My heart's palpitating.

NATÁLIA: I've noticed that the sportsmen who argue most don't understand the first thing about hunting.

LÓMOV: Madam, pleeeease, keep quiet...My heart's bursting....(Shouts.) Keep quiet!

NATÁLIA: I won't keep quiet until you admit that Leap is a hundred times superior to your Guess!

LÓMOV: He's a hundred times inferior. Someone ought to shoot him. My temples...my eyes...my shoulder...

NATÁLIA: No one has to wish that idiotic mutt of yours dead, because he's just skin and bones anyway.

LÓMOV: Keep quiet! I'm having heart failure!

NATÁLIA: I will not keep quiet!

SCENE VII

CHOOBOOKÓV (entering): What's going on now?

NATÁLIA: Papa, tell me, honestly and sincerely: which is the better dog—our Leap or his Guess?

LÓMOV: Stepán Stepánovich, I beseech you, just tell me one thing: is your Leap pug-jawed or isn't he? Yes or no?

CHOOBOOKÓV: So what! Who cares? He's still the best hound in the country, and what not.

LÓMOV: And my Guess isn't better? Tell the truth.

CHOOBOOKÓV: Don't get all worked up, old boy.... Let me explain....Your Guess does have a few good qualities....He's pure-bred, he's got solid legs, he's well put together, and what not. But if you must know, my good man, your dog's got two basic faults: he's old, and his muzzle's too short.

LÓMOV: Excuse me, my heart's racing madly.... Let's examine the facts....Please don't forget that when we were hunting in the Mapooskin Fields, my Guess ran neck and neck with the count's dog Waggy, while your Leap lagged behind by half a mile.

CHOOBOOKÓV: That was because the count's assistant struck him with his riding crop.

LÓMOV: Naturally. All the other dogs were chasing the fox, but yours started running after sheep.

CHOOBOOKÓV: That's a lie! My dear boy, I fly off the handle easily so please let's stop arguing. The man whipped him because people are always envious of everyone else's dogs. Yes, they're all filled with spite! And you sir, are no exception. Why, the minute you notice that anyone else's dog is better than your Guess, you instantly start up something or other...and what not. I've got the memory of an elephant!

LÓMOV: And so do I.

CHOOBOOKÓV (mimicking him): "And so do I."... And what does your memory tell you?

LÓMOV: My heart's palpitating....My foot's paralyzed....I can't anymore...

NATÁLIA (mimicking): "My heart's palpitating..." What kind of hunter are you anyway? You ought to be home in bed catching cockroaches instead of out hunting foxes. Palpitations!...

CHOOBOOKÓV: That's right, what kind of hunter are you? If you've got palpitations, stay home; don't go wobbling around the countryside on horseback. It wouldn't be so bad if you really hunted, but you only tag along in order to start arguments or meddle with other people's dogs, and what not. We'd better stop, I fly off the handle easily. You, sir, are not a hunter, and that's that.

LÓMOV: And you are, I suppose. The only reason you go hunting is to flatter the count and carry on your backstabbing little intrigues....Oh, my heart! ...You schemer!

CHOOBOOKÓV: Me, a schemer. (Shouting.) Shut up!

LÓMOV: Schemer!

CHOOBOOKÓV: Upstart! Pipsqueak!

LÓMOV: You old fogy! You hypocrite!

CHOOBOOKÓV: Shut up, or I'll blast you with a shotgun like a partridge.

LÓMOV: The whole county knows that—Oh, my heart!—your late wife used to beat you....My leg ...my temples...I see stars...I'm falling, falling...

CHOOBOOKÓV: And your housekeeper henpecks you all over the place!

LÓMOV: There, you see...my heart's burst! My shoulder's torn off....Where's my shoulder?...I'm dying! (*Collapses into armchair.*) Get a doctor! (*Faints.*)

CHOOBOOKÓV: Pipsqueak. Weakling. Windbag. I feel sick. (*Drinks some water.*) I feel sick.

NATÁLIA: What kind of hunter are you anyway? You don't even know how to sit in a saddle! (*To her father*) Papa! What's the matter with him? Papa! Look, Papa! (*Screams.*) Iván Vassílievich! He's dead!

CHOOBOOKÓV: I feel sick!...I can't breathe!... Air!

NATÁLIA: He's dead! (*Tugs at* LÓMOV'S *sleeve.*) Iván Vassílievich! Iván Vassílievich! What've we done? He's dead. (*Collapses into easy chair.*) Get a doctor. (*She becomes hysterical.*)

CHOOBOOKÓV: Oh!...What is it? What's wrong?

NATÁLIA (*moaning*): He's dead...he's dead!

CHOOBOOKÓV: Who's dead? (*Glancing at* LÓMOV.) He really is dead, Oh, my God! Get some water! Get a doctor! (*Holds a glass to* LÓMOV'S *mouth.*) Go ahead and drink!...He won't drink....I guess he's dead and so on....Why does everything have to happen to me? Why didn't I put a bullet through my head long ago? Why didn't I cut my throat? What am I waiting for? Give me a knife! Give me a gun!

(LÓMOV *stir.*)

He's reviving, I think....Drink some water!...That's right.

LÓMOV: Stars...fog...where am I?

CHOOBOOKÓV: You two'd better hurry up and get married...Dammit! She accepts....(*Joins* LÓMOV'S *hand with* NATÁLIA'S.) She accepts....My blessings and so forth....Just do me a favor and leave me in peace.

LÓMOV: What? (*Getting up.*) Who?

CHOOBOOKÓV: She accepts. Well? Kiss her and... the two of you can go straight to hell.

NATÁLIA: (*moaning*): He's alive. . . . I accept, I accept....

CHOOBOOKÓV: Kiss and make up.

LÓMOV: What? Who? (*Kisses* NATÁLIA.) *Enchanté* ...Excuse me, but what's going on? Oh yes, I remember. . . . My heart . . . stars . . . I'm very happy, Natália Stepánovna. (*Kisses her hands.*) My leg's paralyzed....

NATÁLIA: I...I'm very happy, too....

CHOOBOOKÓV: That's a load off my back....Whew!

NATÁLIA: But...all the same, why don't you finally admit that Guess isn't as good as Leap.

LÓMOV: He's much better.

NATÁLIA: He's worse.

CHOOBOOKÓV: The launching of marital bliss! Champagne!

LÓMOV: He's better.

NATÁLIA: Worse! Worse! Worse!

CHOOBOOKÓV: (*trying to outshout them*): Champagne! Champagne!

Juan Ramón Jiménez

1881-1958

PLATERO AND I
EXCERPT

He used to come sometimes, lean and panting, to the garden house. The poor thing was always running from someone, accustomed to shouts and stones. Even other dogs snarled at him. And he would go back in the noonday sun, slow and sad, down the hill.

That afternoon he had followed Diana. As I was coming out, the keeper, who on an evil impulse had aimed his gun, fired at him. I had no time to stop him. The wretched dog, with the bullet in his body, whirled dizzily for a moment with a round sharp howl, and fell dead under an acacia bush.

Platero, head erect, kept his eyes fixed on the dog. Diana was frightened and kept trying to hide behind one or the other of us. The keeper, perhaps in remorse, repeated long explanations to no one in particular, angry and helpless in this effort to silence his conscience. A veil had the sun, as in mourning, a large veil, like the tiny one that clouded the one good eye of the murdered dog.

Beaten to exhaustion by the sea wind, the eucalyptus wept ever more loudly toward the storm in the deep crushing silence that noon spread above the dead dog throughout the yet golden countryside.

Translated by Eloise Roach

There is sorrow enough in the natural way
From men and women to fill our day;
But when we are certain of sorrow in store,
Why do we always arrange for more?
Brothers and sisters, I bid you beware
Of giving your heart to a dog to tear.

Rudyard Kipling

Eric Knight

1897-1943

LASSIE
COME-HOME

The dog had met the boy by the school gate for five years. Now she couldn't understand that times were changed and she wasn't supposed to be there any more. But the boy knew.

So when he opened the door of the cottage, he spoke before he entered.

"Mother," he said, "Lassie's come home again."

He waited a moment, as if in hope of something. But the man and woman inside the cottage did not speak.

"Come in, Lassie," the boy said.

He held open the door, and the tricolor collie walked in obediently. Going head down, as a collie will when it knows something is wrong, it went to the rug and lay down before the hearth, a black-white-and-gold aristocrat. The man, sitting on a low stool by the fireside, kept his eyes turned away. The woman went to the sink and busied herself there.

"She were waiting at school for me, just like always," the boy went on. He spoke fast, as if racing against time. "She must ha' got away again. I thought, happen this time, we might just——"

"No!" the woman exploded.

The boy's carelessness dropped. His voice rose in pleading.

"But this time, mother! Just this time. We could hide her. They wouldn't never know."

"Dogs, dogs, dogs!" the woman cried. The words poured from her as if the boy's pleading had been a signal gun for her own anger. "I'm sick o' hearing about tykes round this house. Well, she's sold and gone and done with, so the quicker she's taken back the better. Now get her back quick, or first thing ye know we'll have Hynes round here again. Mr. Hynes!"

Her voice sharpened in imitation of the Cockney accent of the south: "Hi know you Yorkshiremen and yer come-'ome dogs. Training yer dogs to come 'ome so's yer can sell 'em hover and hover again.

"Well, she's sold, so ye can take her out o' my house and home to them as bought her!"

The boy's bottom lip crept out stubbornly, and there was silence in the cottage. Then the dog lifted its head and nudged the man's hand, as a dog will when asking for patting. But the man drew away and stared, silently, into the fire.

The boy tried again, with the ceaseless guile of a child, his voice coaxing.

"Look, feyther, she wants thee to bid her welcome. Aye, she's that glad to be home. Happen they don't tak' good care on her up there? Look, her coat's a bit poorly, don't ye think? A bit o' linseed strained through her drinking water—that's what I'd gi' her."

Still looking in the fire, the man nodded. But the woman, as if perceiving the boy's new attack, sniffed.

"Aye, tha wouldn't be a Carraclough if tha didn't know more about tykes nor breaking eggs wi' a stick. Nor a Yorkshireman. My goodness, it seems to me sometimes that chaps in this village thinks more on their tykes nor they do o' their own flesh and blood. They'll sit by their firesides and let their own bairns starve as long as t' dog gets fed."

The man stirred, suddenly, but the boy cut in quickly.

"But she does look thin. Look, truly—they're not feeding her right. Just look!"

"Aye," the woman chattered. "I wouldn't put it past Hynes to steal t' best part o' t' dog meat for himself. And Lassie always was a strong eater."

"She's fair thin now," the boy said.

Almost unwillingly the man and woman looked at the dog for the first time.

"My gum, she is off a bit," the woman said. Then she caught herself. "Ma goodness, I suppose I'll have to fix her a bit o' summat. She can do wi' it. But soon as she's fed, back she goes. And never another dog I'll have in my house. Never another. Cooking and nursing for 'em, and as much trouble to bring up as a bairn!"

So, grumbling and chattering as a village woman will, she moved about, warming a pan of food for the dog. The man and boy watched the collie eat. When it was done, the boy took from the mantelpiece a folded cloth and a brush, and began prettying the collie's coat. The man watched for several minutes and then could stand it no longer.

"Here," he said.

He took the cloth and brush from the boy and began working expertly on the dog, rubbing the rich, deep coat, then brushing the snowy whiteness of the full ruff and the apron, bringing out the heavy leggings on the forelegs. He lost himself in his work, and the boy sat on the rug, watching contentedly. The woman stood it as long as she could.

"Now will ye please tak' that tyke out o' here?"

The man flared in anger.

"Well, ye wouldn't have me tak' her back looking like a mucky Monday wash, wouldta?"

He bent again, and began fluffing out the collie's petticoats.

"Joe!" the woman pleaded. "Will ye tak' her out

o' here? Hynes'll be nosing round afore ye know it. And I won't have that man in my house. Wearing his hat inside, and going on like he's the duke himself—him and his leggings!"

"All right, lass."

"And this time, Joe, tak' young Joe wi' ye."

"What for?"

"Well, let's get the business done and over with. It's him that Lassie runs away for. She comes for young Joe. So if he went wi' thee, and told her to stay, happen she'd be content and not run away no more, and then we'd have a little peace and quiet in the home—though heaven knows there's not much hope o' that these days, things being like they are."

The woman's voice trailed away, as if she would soon cry in weariness.

The man rose. "Come, Joe," he said. "Get thy cap."

The Duke of Rudling walked along the gravel paths of his place with his granddaughter, Philippa. Philippa was a bright and knowing young woman, allegedly the only member of the duke's family he could address in unspotted language. For it was also alleged that the duke was the most irascible, vile-tempered old man in the three Ridings of Yorkshire.

"Country going to pot!" the duke roared, stabbing at the walk with his great blackthorn stick. "When I was a young man! Hah! Women today not as pretty. Horses today not as fast. As for dogs—ye don't see dogs today like——"

Just then the duke and Philippa came round a clump of rhododendrons and saw a man, a boy and a dog.

"Ah," said the duke, in admiration. Then his brow knotted. "Damme, Carraclough! What're ye doing with my dog?"

He shouted it quite as if the others were in the next county, for it was also the opinion of the Duke of Rudling that people were not nearly so keen of hearing as they used to be when he was a young man.

"It's Lassie," Carraclough said. "She runned away again and I brought her back."

Carraclough lifted his cap, and poked the boy to do the same, not in any servile gesture, but to show that they were as well brought up as the next.

"Damme, ran away again!" the duke roared. "And I told that utter nincompoop Hynes to—where is he? Hynes! Hynes! Damme, Hynes, what're ye hiding for?"

"Coming, your lordship!" sounded a voice, far away behind the shrubberies. And soon Hynes appeared, a sharp-faced man in check coat, riding breeches, and the cloth leggings that grooms wear.

"Take this dog," roared the duke, "and pen her up! And, damme, if she breaks out again, I'll—

The duke waved his great stick threateningly, and then, without so much as a thank you or kiss the back of my hand to Joe Carraclough, he went stamping and muttering away.

"I'll pen 'er up," Hynes muttered, when the duke was gone. "And if she ever gets awye agyne, I'll——"

He made as if to grab the dog, but Joe Carraclough's hobnailed boot trod heavily on Hynes foot.

"I brought my lad wi' me to bid her stay, so we'll pen her up this time. Eigh—sorry! I didn't see I were on thy foot. Come, Joe, lad."

They walked down the crunching gravel path, along by the neat kennel buildings. When Lassie was behind the closed door, she raced into the high wire run where she could see them as they went. She pressed close against the wire, waiting.

The boy stood close, too, his fingers through the meshes touching the dog's nose.

"Go on, lad," his father ordered. "Bid her stay!"

The boy looked around, as if for help that he did not find. He swallowed, and then spoke, low and quickly.

"Stay here, Lassie, and don't come home no more," he said. "And don't come to school for me no more. Because I don't want to see ye no more. 'Cause tha's a bad dog, and we don't love thee no more, and we don't want thee. So stay there forever and leave us be, and don't never come home no more."

Then he turned, and because it was hard to see the path plainly, he stumbled. But his father, who was holding his head very high as they walked away from Hynes, shook him savagely, and snapped roughly: "Look where tha's going!"

Then the boy trotted beside his father. He was thinking that he'd never be able to understand why grownups sometimes were so bad-tempered with you, just when you needed them most.

After that, there were days and days that passed, and the dog did not come to the school gate any more. So then it was not like old times. There were so many things that were not like old times.

The boy was thinking that as he came wearily up the path and opened the cottage door and heard his father's voice, tense with anger: "...walk my feet off. If tha thinks I like——"

Then they heard his opening of the door and the voice stopped and the cottage was silent.

That's how it was now, the boy thought. They stopped talking in front of you. And this, somehow, was too much for him to bear.

He closed the door, ran out into the night, and onto the moor, that great flat expanse of land where all the people of that village walked in lonesomeness when life and its troubles seemed past bearing.

A long while later, his father's voice cut through the darkness.

"What's tha doing out here, Joe lad?"

"Walking."

"Aye."

They went on together, aimlessly, each following his own thoughts. And they both thought about the dog that had been sold.

"That maun't think we're hard on thee, Joe," the man said at last. "It's just that a chap's got to be honest. There's that to it. Sometimes, when a chap doesn't have much, he clings right hard to what he's got. And honest is honest, and there's no two ways about it.

"Why, look, Joe. Seventeen year I worked in that Clarabelle Pit till she shut down, and a good collier too. Seventeen year! And butties I've had by the dozen, and never a man of 'em can ever say that Joe Carraclough kept what wasn't his, nor spoke what wasn't true. Not a man in this Riding can ever call a Carraclough mishonest.

"And when ye've sold a man summat, and ye've taken his brass, and ye've spent it—well, then done's done. That's all. And ye've got to stand by that."

"But Lassie was——"

"Now, Joe! Ye can't alter it, ever. It's done—and happen it's for t' best. No two ways, Joe, she were getting hard to feed. Why, ye wouldn't want Lassie to be going around getting peaked and pined, like some chaps round here keep their tykes. And if ye're fond of her, then just think on it that now she's got lots to eat, and a private kennel, and a good run to herself, and living like a varritable princess, she is. Ain't that best for her?"

"We wouldn't pine her. We've always got lots to eat."

The man blew out his breath, angrily, "Eigh, Joe, nowt pleases thee. Well then, tha might as well have it. Tha'll never see Lassie no more. She run home once too often, so the duke's taken her wi' him up to his place in Scotland, and there she'll stay. So it's good-by and good luck to her, and she'll never come home no more, she won't. Now, I weren't off to tell thee, but there it is, so put it in thy pipe and smoke it, and let's never say a word about it no more—especially in front of thy mother."

The boy stumbled on in the darkness. Then the man halted.

"We ought to be getting back, lad. We left thy mother alone."

He turned the boy about, and then went on, but as if he were talking to himself.

"Tha sees, Joe, women's not like men. They have to stay home and manage best they can, and just spend the time in wishing. And when things don't go right, well, they have to take it out in talk and give a man hell. But it don't mean nowt, really, so tha shouldn't mind when they mother talks hard.

"Ye just got to learn to be patient and let 'em talk, and just let it go up t' chimney wi' th' smoke."

Then they were quiet, until, over the rise, they saw the lights of the village. Then the boy spoke: "How far away is Scotland, feyther?"

"Nay, lad, it's a long, long road."

"But how far, feyther?"

"I don't know—but it's a longer road than thee or me'll ever walk. Now, lad. Don't fret no more, and try to be a man—and don't plague they mother no more, wilta?"

Joe Carraclough was right. It is a long road, as they say in the North, from Yorkshire to Scotland. Much too far for a man to walk—or a boy. And though the boy often thought of it, he remembered his father's words on the moor, and he put the thought behind him.

But there is another way of looking at it; and that's the distance from Scotland to Yorkshire. And that is just as far as from Yorkshire to Scotland. A matter of about four hundred miles, it would be, from the Duke of Rudling's place far up in the Highlands, to the village of Holdersby. That would be for a man, who could go fairly straight.

To an animal, how much farther would it be? For a dog can study no maps, read no signposts, ask no directions. It could only go blindly, by instinct, knowing that it must keep on to the south, to the south. It would wander and err, quest and quarter, run into firths and lochs that would send it side-tracking and back-tracking before it could go again on its way—south.

A thousand miles, it would be, going that way—a thousand miles over strange terrain.

There would be moors to cross, and burns to swim. And then those great, long lochs that stretch almost from one side of that dour land to another, would bar the way and send a dog questing a hundred miles before it could find a crossing that would allow it to go south.

And, too, there would be rivers to cross, wide rivers like the Forth and the Clyde, the Tweed and the Tyne, where one must go miles to find bridges. And the bridges would be in towns. And in the towns there would be officials—like the one in Lanarkshire. In all his life he had never let a captured dog get away—except one. That one was a gaunt, snarling collie that whirled on him right in the pound itself, and fought and twisted loose to race away down the city street—going south.

But there are also kind people, too; ones knowing

and understanding in the ways of dogs. There was an old couple in Durham who found a dog lying exhausted in a ditch one night—lying there with its head to the south. They took that dog into their cottage and warmed it and fed it and nursed it. And because it seemed an understanding, wise dog, they kept it in their home, hoping it would learn to be content. But, as it grew stronger, every afternoon toward four o'clock it would go to the door and whine, and then begin pacing back and forth between the door and the window, back and forth as the animals do in their cages at the zoo.

They tried every wile and every kindness to make it bide with them, but finally, when to dog began to refuse food, the old people knew what they must do. Because they understood dogs, they opened the door one afternoon and they watched a collie go, not down the road to the right, or to the left, but straight across a field toward the south; going steadily at a trot, as if it knew it still had a long, long road to travel.

Ah, a thousand miles of tor and brae, of shire and moor, of path and road and plowland, of river and stream and burn and brook and beck, of snow and rain and fog and sun, is a long way, even for a human being. But it would seem too far—much, much too far—for any dog to travel blindly and win through.

And yet—and yet—who shall say why, when so many weeks had passed that hope against hope was dying, a boy coming out of school, out of the cloakroom that always smelled of damp wool drying, across the concrete play yard with the black, waxed slides, should turn his eyes to a spot by the school gate from force of five years of habit, and see there a dog? Not a dog, this one, that lifted glad ears above a proud, slim head with its black-and-gold mask; but a dog that lay weakly, trying to lift a head that would no longer lift, trying to wag a tail that was torn and blotched and matted with dirt and burs, and managing to do nothing much except to whine in a weak, happy, crying way as a boy on his knees threw arms about it, and hands touched it that had not touched it for many a day.

Then who shall picture the urgency of a boy, running, awkwardly, with a great dog in his arms—running through the village, past the empty mill, past the Labor Exchange, where the men looked up from their deep ponderings on life and the dole? Or who shall describe the high tones of a voice—a boy's voice, calling as he runs up a path: "Mother! Oh, mother! Lassie's come home! Lassie's come home!"

Nor does anyone who ever owned a dog need to be told the sounds a man makes as he bends over a dog that has been his for many years; nor how a woman moves quickly, preparing food—which might be the family's condensed milk stirred into warm water; nor how the jowl of a dog is lifted so that raw egg and brandy, bought with precious pence, should be spooned in; nor how bleeding pads are bandaged, tenderly.

That was one day. There was another day when the woman in the cottage sighed with pleasure, for a dog lifted itself to its feet for the first time to stand over a bowl of oatmeal, putting its head down and lapping again and again while its pinched flanks quivered.

And there was another day when the boy realized that, even now, the dog was not to be his again. So the cottage rang again with protests and cries, and a woman shrilling: "Is there never to be no more peace in my house and home?" Long after he was in bed that night the boy heard the rise and fall of the woman's voice, and the steady, reiterative tone of the man's. It went on long after he was asleep.

In the morning the man spoke, not looking at the boy, saying the words as if he had long rehearsed them.

"Thy mother and me have decided upon it that Lassie shall stay here till she's better. Anyhow, nobody could nurse her better than us. But the day that t' duke comes back, then back she goes, too. For she belongs to him, and that's honest, too. Now tha has her for a while, so be content."

In childhood, "for a while" is such a great stretch of days when seen from one end. It is a terribly short time seen from the other.

The boy knew how short it was that morning as he went to school and saw a motorcar driven by a young woman. And in the car was a gray-thatched, terrible old man, who waved a cane and shouted: "Hi! Hi, there! Damme, lad! You there! Hi!"

Then it was no use running, for the car could go faster than you, and soon it was beside you and the man was saying; "Damme, Philippa, will you make this smelly thing stand still a moment! Hi, lad!"

"Yes, sir."

"You're What's-is-Name's lad, aren't you?"

"Ma feyther's Joe Carraclough."

"I know. I know. Is he home now?"

"No, sir. He's away to Allerby. A mate spoke for him at the pit and he's gone to see if there's a chance."

"When'll he be back?"

"I don't know. I think about tea."

"Eh, yes. Well, yes. I'll drop round about fivish to see that father of yours. Something important."

It was hard to pretend to listen to lessons. There was only waiting for noon. Then the boy ran home.

"Mother! T' duke is back and he's coming to take Lassie away."

"Eigh, drat my buttons. Never no peace in this house. Is tha sure?"

"Aye. He stopped me. He said tell feyther he'll be round at five. Can't we hide her? Oh, mother."

"Nay, thy feyther——"

"Won't you beg him? Please, please. Beg feyther to——"

"Young Joe, now it's no use. So stop thy teasing! Thy feyther'll not lie. That much I'll give him. Come good, come bad, he'll not lie."

"But just this once, mother. Please beg him, just this once. Just one lie wouldn't hurt him. I'll make it up to him. I will. When I'm growed up, I'll get a job. I'll make money. I'll buy him things—and you, too. I'll buy you both anything you want if you'll only——"

For the first time in his trouble the boy became a child, and the mother, looking over, saw the tears that ran openly down his contorted face. She turned her face to the fire, and there was a pause. Then she spoke.

"Joe, tha mustn't," she said softly. "Tha must learn never to want nothing in life like that. It don't do, lad. Tha mustn't want things bad, like tha wants Lassie."

The boy shook his clenched fists in impatience.

"It ain't that, mother. Ye don't understand. Don't ye see—it ain't me that wants her. It's her that wants us! That's what made her come all them miles. It's her that wants us, so terrible bad!"

The woman turned and stared. If was as if, in that moment, she were seeing this child, this boy, this son of her own, for the first time in many years. She turned her head down toward the table. It was surrender.

"Come and eat, then," she said. "I'll talk to him. I will that, all right, I feel sure he won't lie. But I'll talk to him, all right. I'll talk to Mr. Joe Carraclough. I will indeed!"

At five that afternoon, the Duke of Rudling, fuming and muttering, got out of a car at a cottage gate to find a boy barring his way. This was a boy who stood, stubbornly, saying fiercely: "Away wi' thee! Thy tyke's net here!"

"Damme, Philippa, th' lad's touched," the duke said. "He is, he's touched."

Scowling and thumping his stick, the old duke advanced until the boy gave way, backing down the path out of the reach of the waving blackthorn stick.

"Thy tyke's net here," the boy protested.

"What's he saying?" the girl asked.

"Says my dog isn't here. Damme, you going deaf? I'm supposed to be deaf, and I hear him plainly enough. Now, ma lad, what tyke o' mine's net here?"

As he turned to the boy, the duke spoke in broadest Yorkshire, as he did always to the people of the cottages—a habit which the Duchess of Rudling, and many more members of the duke's family, deplored.

"Coom, coom, ma lad. Whet tyke's net here?"

"No tyke o' thine. Us hasn't got it." The words began running faster and faster as the boy backed away from the fearful old man who advanced. "No tyke could have done it. No tyke can come all them miles. It isn't Lassie. It's another one that looks like her. It isn't Lassie!"

"Why, bless ma heart and sowl," the duke puffed. "Where's thy father, ma lad?"

The door behind the boy opened, and a woman's voice spoke.

"If it's Joe Carraclough ye want, he's out in the shed—and been there shut up half the afternoon."

"What's this lad talking about—a dog of mine being here?"

"Nay," the woman snapped quickly. "He didn't say a tyke o' thine was here. He said it wasn't here."

"Well, what dog o' mine isn't here, then?"

The woman swallowed, and looked about as if for help. The duke stood, peering from under his jutting eyebrows. Her answer, truth or lie, was never spoken, for then they heard the rattle of a door opening, and a man making a pursing sound with his lips, as he will when he wants a dog to follow, and then Joe Carraclough's voice said: "This is t' only tyke us has here. Does it look like any dog that belongs to thee?"

With his mouth opening to cry one last protest, the boy turned. And his mouth stayed open. For there he saw his father, Joe Carraclough, the collie fancier, standing with a dog at his heels—a dog that sat at his left heel patiently, as any well-trained dog should do—as Lassie used to do. But this dog was not Lassie. In fact, it was ridiculous to think of it at the same moment as you thought of Lassie.

For where Lassie's skull was aristocratic and slim, this dog's head was clumsy and rough. Where Lassie's ears stood in twin-lapped symmetry, this dog had one ear draggling and the other standing up Alsatian fashion in a way to give any collie breeder the cold shivers. Where Lassie's coat was rich tawny gold, this dog's coat had ugly patches of black; and where Lassie's apron was a billowing stretch of snow-white, this dog had puddles of off-color blue-merle mixture. Besides, Lassie had four white paws, and this one had one paw white, two dirty-brown, and one almost black.

That is the dog they all looked at as Joe Carraclough stood there, having told no lie, having only asked a question. They all stood, waiting the duke's verdict.

But the duke said nothing. He only walked forward, slowly, as if he were seeing a dream. He bent beside the collie, looking with eyes that were as knowing about dogs as any Yorkshireman alive. And those eyes did not waste themselves upon twisted ears, or blotched marking, or rough head. Instead they were looking at a paw that the duke lifted, looked at the underneath side of the paw, staring intently at five black pads, crossed and recrossed with the scars where thorns had lacerated, and stones had torn.

For a long time the duke stared, and when he got up he did not speak in Yorkshire accents any more. He spoke as a gentleman should, and he said: "Joe Carraclough. I never owned this dog. 'Pon my soul, she's never belonged to me. Never!"

Then he turned and went stumping down the path, thumping his cane and saying: "Bless my soul. Four hundred miles! Damme, wouldn't ha' believed it. Damme—five hundred miles!"

He was at the gate when his granddaughter whispered to him fiercely.

"Of course," he cried, "Mind your own business. Exactly what I came for. Talking about dogs made me forget. Carraclough! Carraclough! What're ye hiding for?"

"I'm still here, sir."

"Ah, there you are. You working?"

"Eigh, now. Working," Joe said. That's the best he could manage.

"Yes, working, working!" The duke fumed.

"Well, now——" Joe began.

Then Mrs. Carraclough came to his rescue, as a good housewife in Yorkshire will.

"Why, Joe's got three or four things that he's been considering," she said, with proper display of pride. "But he hasn't quite said yes or no to any of them yet."

"Then say no, quick," the old man puffed. "Had to sack Hynes. Didn't know a dog from a drunken filly. Should ha' known all along no damn Londoner could handle dogs fit for Yorkshire taste. How much, Carraclough?"

"Well, now," Joe began.

"Seven pounds a week, and worth every penny," Mrs. Carraclough chipped in. "One o' them other offers may come up to eight," she lied, expertly. For there's always a certain amount of lying to be done in life, and when a woman's married to a man who has made a lifelong cult of being honest, then she's got to learn to do the lying for two.

"Five," roared the duke—who, after all, was a Yorkshireman, and couldn't help being a bit sharp about things that pertained to money.

"Six," said Mrs. Carraclough.

"Five pound ten," bargained the duke, cannily.

"Done," said Mrs. Carraclough, who would have been willing to settle for three pounds in the first place. "But, o' course, us gets the cottage too."

"All right," puffed the duke. "Five pounds ten and the cottage. Begin Monday. But—on one condition. Carraclough, you can live on my land, but I won't have that thick-skulled, screw-lugged, gray-tailed eyesore of a misshapen mongrel on my property. Now, never let me see her again. You'll get rid of her?"

He waited, and Joe fumbled for words. But it was the boy who answered, happily, gaily: "Oh, no, sir, she'll be waiting at school for me most o' the time. And, anyway, in a day or so we'll have her fixed up and coped up so's ye'd never, never recognize her."

"I don't doubt that," puffed the duke as he went to the car. "I don't doubt ye could do just exactly that."

It was a long time afterward, in the car, that the girl said: "Don't sit there like a lion on the Nelson column. And I thought you were supposed to be a hard man."

"Fiddlesticks, m' dear. I'm a ruthless realist. For five years I've sworn I'd have that dog by hook or crook, and now, egad, at last I've got her."

"Pooh! You had to buy the man before you could get his dog."

"Well, perhaps that's not the worst part of the bargain."

We are going out. You know the pitch of the word,
Probing the tone of thought as it comes through fog
And reaches by devious means
    (half-smelt, half-heard)
The four-legged brain of a walk-ecstatic dog.

Harold Munro

DEFINITION

Dog, *n.* A kind of additional or subsidiary Deity designed to catch the overflow and surplus of the worship. This Divine Being in some of his smaller and silkier incarnations takes, in the affection of Woman, the place to which there is no human male aspirant. The Dog is a survival—an anachronism. He toils not, neither does he spin, yet Solomon in all his glory never lay upon a door-mat all day long, sun-soaked and fly-fed and fat, while his master worked for the means wherewith to purchase an idle wag of the Solomonic tail, seasoned with a look of tolerant recognition.

The Devil's Dictionary, Ambrose Bierce

Rupert Brooke

1877-1915

THE LITTLE
DOG'S DAY

All in the town were still asleep,
When the sun came up with a shout and a leap.
In the lonely streets unseen by man,
A little dog danced. And the day began.

All his life he'd been good, as far as he could,
And the poor little beast had done all that he should.
But this morning he swore, by Odin and Thor
And the Canine Valhalla—he'd stand it no more!

So his prayer he got granted—to do just what he
    wanted,
Prevented by none, for the space of one day.
"*Jam incipiebo, sedere facebo,*"
In dog-Latin he quoth, "*Euge! sophos! hurray!*"

He fought with the he-dogs, and winked at the
    she-dogs.

A thing that had never been *heard* of before.
"For the stigma of gluttony, I care not a button!" he
Cried, and ate all he could swallow—and more.

He took sinewy lumps from the shins of old frumps,
And mangled the errand-boys—when he could
    get 'em.
He shammed furious *rabies,* and bit all the babies,
And followed the cats up the trees, and then ate 'em!

They thought 'twas the devil was holding a revel,
And sent for the parson to drive him away;
For the town never knew such a hullabaloo
As that little dog raised—till the end of that day.

When the blood-red sun had gone burning down,
And the lights were lit in the little town,
Outside, in the gloom of the twilight grey,
The little dog died when he'd had his day.

Johann Wilhelm Klein

Nineteenth Century

TEXTBOOK
FOR TEACHING
THE BLIND
Published in Vienna. 1819

In an institute for the blind, dogs can also be prepared to serve as guides to such of the blind as are accustomed to walk about.

For this, the poodle and shepherd dogs are the most useful.

From the collar of the dog extends either a strap or a stick which is grasped by the left hand of the blind person, who also uses a cane in the right hand.

The rigid stick must run through a loose brace around the body of the dog, so that a side movement of the animal is fully felt in the hands of the blind person. The guiding stick is arranged with a crossbar in such a manner that it can easily be fastened to the collar of the dog; and it also has, near the top, a loop, so that the hand of the blind person will not easily lose its grip.

This use of a guiding stick has the advantage that the blind person notices at once when the dog is standing still, which is not true when he is led by a strap.

The training of the dogs, at least in the beginning, must be done by a sighted person. One leads him, many times, on the same road and drills him, particular attention being paid to places where through turning, through slow pace, through standing still, or through other movements which might be useful to the blind in situations such as the turning of the street and in the avoidance of obstacles that lie ahead—through all this the dog will be made alert to various kinds of danger situations.

Then the blind person takes the dog in hand himself and goes with him, at first on the same road with which he is already acquainted, in order to become accustomed to the movements and signals of the animal.

It is obvious that from now on the dog will be fed and cared for by the blind person himself, in order to arrive at a mutual understanding and to establish a true and faithful attachment with the leader dog.

Jacob Birrer

Nineteenth Century

A BLIND MAN
TEACHES
HIS DOG
Published in Germany. 1845

Probably among all the domestic animals that serve man there is none which performs as many services as the dog; nor is there any animal as attached to man as this faithful guardian and companion. The dog excels in activity and intelligence as well as in attachment and obedience, and has such a good-natured character, that apparently he recalls only the kind deeds and not the whippings. Whatever his master orders him to do he carries out without tiring; anything entrusted to him he guards with the greatest care: if we are in danger he stands by to help us: he even avenges his master and helps to give the affronter over to deserved punishment.

Especially for the blind this animal performs most effective services: he functions excellently for those who have been robbed of their eyesight. One can say that the dog which serves as a guide to these unfortunate ones fulfills a mission which places him at the head of his kind. But for this he ought to be trained with special care and by the blind person himself.

I feel it a duty therefore to my blind colleagues who want to be guided by dogs, to give instructions, based largely on my own practical experiences, for training the dogs. Some four or five years ago I learned that in Paris many a blind person has a poodle as a guide, but I could not entirely believe it. At that time I did not want a dog as a guide; but about two years ago I had the idea that I would try an experiment with a Spitz.

I did my training in the following manner:

1. I always saw to it that the dog went ahead of me while I held the leash: if he did this quite regularly I went after a while to some place well known to me in order to find out whether he kept his path faithfully.

2. If I were sure of that, I took him to a row of trees and walked up and down. If the dog led me so near a tree that I was in danger of hitting it I went on the other side of the tree and pulled the leash around the trunk until the dog felt some pain, in order to make him avoid trees, stones, etc.

3. When I was certain that he could lead me along a row of trees without my hitting them I went to an avenue where I knew there were barriers or holes in the street; and there I continued the same exercises as above with the dog. This is one of the most difficult tasks, for it is necessary to be very careful to see that the dog really goes along the avenue instead of skirting around it. Only with great patience can this goal be achieved; so if the dog has learned his lesson his teacher may well show him some favor to signalize success. This training must be repeated a number of times, and if the dog does not seem to grasp what is wanted it might be well to pull him into an obstruction and punish him so that he will submit to the will of his master; but do not beat him unless it is absolutely necessary. In like manner one can proceed in a roomy apartment.

4. Generally speaking dogs like to go outdoors and often cannot wait until the door is opened for them to leap and bound outside; but for a blind person this may cause considerable embarrassment so I did the following with my dog. I placed a bench in the outer hall but in such a manner that on one side a small opening was left to get through; then I put the leash on before I even opened the door so he would be unable to dart out. Thereupon he immediately ran under the bench which I overturned so he might believe that it was his master who had fallen on the floor. The noise frightened the animal and within a short space of time he would find the opening by means of which he could lead me outside.—This particular lesson requires frequent repetition!—In a similar fashion the dog can be made attentive to the shafts on carriages, wagons, etc.; but the blind

person must know precisely where these shafts may be since they are commonly breast high. If the dog does not pay attention to the height of these objects, which is difficult for him to do, one ought to pull him up by the leash and punish him until he has an idea of what is wanted.

5. I then take him to a safe street where there are no brooks, bridges, or banks or other dangerous places. If a vehicle approached I pulled on the leash, about twenty or thirty steps before necessary, as a sign that he must evade by going either to the right or left footpath; and he learns very quickly that in such circumstances he must take the safe path. When he has accustomed himself to this sign one may take him from the known road to an unknown one and there continue the training. If, for example, I walked for half-an-hour and learned that half way two streets forked: I must give the sign sufficiently in advance so that he would not start down the wrong way. If he should retrace this route without paying attention, one turns back and repeats the signal until he understands it. One might use the same method in cities that have side streets and abutting houses.

6. If I am going into a house, the dog relaxes the leash somewhat and stands still in front of the steps

until he notices that I have reached them with the help of my cane; somewhat the same is done on leaving the house. Also I try to accustom him to go directly to the doorway itself and not stand behind the doors. In the same way I then walked over small boardwalks or bridges over brooks and rivers, where likewise by relaxing the leash he gave me the sign so that I could seek out the safe place by means of my cane, whereupon the dog went very slowly in front of me until I was again on safe ground.

Just to say a word about the poodle; I am ready to admit that this is the best species for training since they can also be taught other amusing tricks; but they require a special type of training. While a spitz has staying powers even on long tours, the poodle can be used only in cities and even there is not much more than a lap dog; in addition in summer it is apt to be lazy. The poodle is very sensitive and does not react well to punishment. Also I would prefer the spitz to the poodle not only because it is stronger but also because it is more easily trained; only one must be careful to see that the animal is no more than ten or, at the most, sixteen months old, and in order to avoid embarrassments it had better be a male.

Abram V. Courtney

Nineteenth Century

MY FAITHFUL DOG "CAPER"

I therefore left the Perkins Institute for the Blind as it appeared to me more proper to gain my living by my own industry rather than to eat the bread of charity.... (Although) I have at times accepted the aid that my misfortune has rendered necessary, I have never degraded myself by asking alms.... My faithful dog, Caper, (which I acquired in Bangor, Maine in 1851) with care leads me around corners and across streets, always apprising me of approaching danger, by pulling me back, and will not move, even though I scold him severely. His instinct is remarkable; he seems to understand what I say. If I tell him I want to go to the barber's, he leads me to the place, or he will lead me to any other place where he is in the habit of going, without difficulty or mistake; nor will he leave me for a moment, unless I tell him....

Caper, the dog who for years has been the constant partner of my wanderings, is one of the most intelligent and affectionate of his race. To me he has always been a friend indeed; always patient, submissive, careful and trustworthy. He understands the misfortune of his master, and comprehends the responsibility which devolves upon him as my guide and guard. Caper claims kindred both from the Newfoundland and Spaniel breed of dogs.... Since then he has accompanied me in my travels through nearly all of the Northern States; and has served me in the capacity of guide, companion, bodyguard and monitor. Upon one occasion, when laden with a number of heavy bundles, I sat down by the roadside for a moment's rest, and upon arising again to renew my weary march, I was surprised to find that my dog did not respond to my order to go on. He sprang upon my knees, whined, barked, and used every effort in his power to make me understand that something was wrong. I was unable to comprehend his meaning until a stranger, passing by, remarked, "Sir, you have left a bundle behind you, on the grass."

Caper is my companion, day and night. He always sleeps in the same room, and allows no one to enter during the night.... He is so fond of his master that he cannot bear to be separated from him.... During the last five years he has proved so trusty a friend, that please God, he shall never be separated from me again while we both live.

Hugh Walpole

1884-1941

THE WHISTLE

Mrs. Penwin gave one of her nervous little screams when she saw the dog.

"Oh Charlie!" she cried. "You surely haven't bought it!" And her little nose, that she tried so fiercely to keep smooth, wrinkled into its customary little guttering of wrinkles.

The dog, taking an instant dislike to her, slunk, his head between his shoulders. He was an Alsatian.

"Well—" said Charlie, smiling nervously. He knew that his impulsiveness had led him once more astray. "Only the other evening you were saying that you'd like another dog."

"Yes, but *not* an Alsatian! You *know* what Alsatians are. We read about them in the paper every day. They are simply *not* to be trusted. I'm sure he looks as vicious as anything. And what about Mopsa?"

"Oh, Mopsa—" Charlie hesitated. "He'll be all right. You see, Sibyl, it was charity really. The Sillons are going to London as you know. They simply can't take him—it wouldn't be fair. They've found it difficult enough in Edinburgh as it is."

"I'm sure they are simply getting rid of him because he's vicious."

"No. Maude Sillon assured me he's like a lamb—"

"Oh, Maude! She'd say anything!"

"You know that you've been wanting a companion for Mopsa—"

"A companion for Mopsa! That's good!" Sibyl laughed her shrill little laugh that was always just out of tune.

"Well, we'll try him. We can easily get rid of him. And Blake shall look after him."

"Blake?" She was scornful. She detested Blake, but he was too good a chauffeur to lose.

"And he's most awfully handsome. You can't deny it."

She looked. Yes, he was most awfully handsome. He had laid down his head on his paws, staring in front of him, quite motionless. He seemed to be waiting scornfully until he should be given his next command. The power in those muscles, moulded under the skin, must be terrific. His long wolf ears lay flat. His color was lovely, here silver gray, there faintly amber. Yes, he was a magnificent dog. A little like Blake in his strength, silence, sulkiness.

She turned again to the note that she was writing.

"We'll try him if you like. Anyway there are no children about. It's Blake's responsibility—and the moment he's tiresome he goes."

Charlie was relieved. It hadn't been so hard after all.

"Oh, Blake says he doesn't mind. In fact he seemed to take to the dog at once. I'll call him."

He went to the double windows that opened into the garden and called: "Blake! Blake!" Blake came. He was still in his chauffeur's uniform, having just driven his master and the dog in from Keswick. He was a very large man, very fair in coloring, plainly of great strength. His expression was absolutely English in its complete absence of curiosity, its certainty that it knew the best about everything, its suspicion, its determination not to be taken in by anybody, and its latent kindliness. He had very blue eyes and was clean-shaven; his cap was in his hand and his hair, which was fair almost to whiteness, lay roughly across his forehead. He was not especially neat but of a quite shining cleanliness.

The dog got up and moved towards him. Both the Penwins were short and slight; they looked now rather absurdly small beside the man and the dog.

"Look here, Blake," said Charlie Penwin, speaking with much authority, "Mrs. Penwin is nervous about the dog. He's your responsibility, mind, and if there's the slightest bit of trouble, he goes. You understand that?"

"Yes, sir," said Blake, looking at the dog, "but there won't be no trouble."

"That's a ridiculous thing to say," remarked Mrs. Penwin sharply, looking up from her note. "How can you be sure, Blake? You know how uncertain Alsatians are. I don't know what Mr. Penwin was thinking about."

Blake said nothing. Once again, and for the hundred-thousandth time, both the Penwins wished that they could pierce him with needles. It was quite terrible the way that Blake didn't speak when expected to, but then he was so wonderful a chauffeur, so good a driver, so excellent a mechanic, so honest—and Clara, his wife, was an admirable cook.

"You'd better take the dog with you now, Blake. What's its name?"

"Adam," said Charlie.

"Adam! What a foolish name for a dog! Now don't disturb Clara with him, Blake. Clara hates to have her kitchen messed up."

Blake, without a word, turned and went, the dog following closely at his heels.

Yes, Clara hated to have her kitchen messed up. She was standing now, her sleeves rolled back, her plump hands and wrists covered with dough. Mopsa, the Sealyham, sat at her side, his eyes, glistening with greed, raised to those doughy arms. But at sight of the Alsatian he turned and flew at his throat.

He was a dog who prided himself on fighting instantly every other dog. With human beings he was mild and indifferently amiable. Children could do what they would with him. He was exceedingly conceited, and cared for no one but himself.

He was clever, however, and hid this indifference from many sentimental human beings.

Blake, with difficulty, separated the two dogs. The Alsatian behaved quite admirably, merely noticing the Sealyham and looking up at Blake to say, "I won't let myself go here although I should like to. I know that you would rather I didn't." The Sealyham, muttering deeply, bore the Alsatian no grudge. He was simply determined that he should have no foothold here.

Torrents of words passed from Clara. She had always as much to say as her husband had little. She said the same thing many times over as though she had an idiot to deal with. She knew that her husband was not an idiot—very far from it—but she had for many years been trying to make some impression on him. Defeated beyond hope, all she could now do was to resort to old and familiar tactics. What was this great savage dog? Where had he come from? Surely the Mistress didn't approve, and she wouldn't have her kitchen messed up, not for anybody, and as Harry (Blake) very well knew, nothing upset her like a dog fight, and if they were going to be perpetual, which, knowing Mopsa's character, they probably would be, she must just go to Mrs. Penwin and tell her that, sorry though she was after being with her all these years, she just couldn't stand it and would have to go, for if there was one thing more than another that really upset her it was a dog fight, and as Harry knew having the kitchen messed up was a thing that she couldn't stand. She paused and began vehemently to roll her dough. She was short and plump with fair hair and blue eyes like her husband's.

When she was excited, little glistening beads of sweat appeared on her forehead. No one in this world knew whether Blake was fond of her or no, Clara Blake least of all. She wondered perpetually; this uncertainty and her cooking were her principal interests in life. There were times when Blake seemed very fond of her indeed, others when he appeared not to be aware that she existed.

All he said now was, "The dog won't be no trouble," and went out, the dog at his heels. The Sealyham thought for a moment that he would follow him, then, with a little sniff of greed, settled himself down again at Clara Blake's feet.

The two went out into the thin, misty autumn sunshine, down through the garden into the garage. The Alsatian walked very closely beside Blake as though some invisible cord held them together. All his life, now two years in length, it had been always his constant principle to attach himself to somebody. For, in this curious world where he was, not his natural world at all, every breath, every movement, rustle of wind, sound of voices, patter of rain, ringing of bells, filled him with nervous alarm. He went always on guard, keeping his secret soul to himself, surrendering nothing, a captive in the country of the enemy. There might exist a human being to whom he would surrender himself. Although he had been attached to several people, he had not in his two years yet found one to whom he could give himself. Now as he trod softly over the amber and rosy leaves he was not sure that this man, beside whom he walked, might not be the one.

In the garage Blake took off his coat, put on his blue overalls and began to work. The dog stretched himself out on the stone floor, his head on his paws and waited. Once and again he started, his pointed ears pricked, at some unexpected sound. A breeze blew the brown leaves up and down in the sun, and the white road beyond the garage pierced like a shinning bone the cloudless sky.

Blake's thoughts ran, as they always did, with slow assurance. This was a fine dog. He'd known the first moment that he set eyes on him that this was the dog for him. At that first glance something in his heart had been satisfied, something that had for years been unfulfilled. For they had had no children, he and Clara, and a motor car was fine to drive and look after, but after all it couldn't give you everything, and he wasn't one to make friends (too damned cautious), and the people he worked for were all right but nothing extra, and he really didn't know whether he cared for Clara or no. It was so difficult after so many years married to tell. There were lots of times when he couldn't sort of see her at all.

He began to take out the spark plugs to clean them. That was the worst of these Daimlers, fine cars, as good as any going, but you had to be forever cleaning the spark plugs. Yes, that dog was a beauty. He was going to take to that dog.

The dog looked at him, stared at him as though he were saying something. Blake looked at the dog. Then, with a deep sigh, as though some matter, for long uncertain, was at last completely settled, the dog rested again his head on his paws, staring in front of him, and so fell asleep. Blake, softly whistling, continued his work.

A very small factor, in itself quite unimportant, can bring into serious conflict urgent forces. So it was now when this dog, Adam, came into the life of the Penwins.

Mrs. Penwin, like so many English wives and unlike all American wives, had never known so much domestic power as she descried. Her husband was, of course, devoted to her, but he was forever just escaping her, escaping her into that world of men that is so important in England, that is, even in these very modern days, still a world in the main apart from women.

Charlie Penwin had not very many opportunities to escape from his wife, and he was glad that he had not, for when they came he took them. His ideal was the ideal of most English married men (and of very few American married men), namely, that he should be a perfect companion to his wife. He fulfilled this ideal; they were excellent companions, the two of them, so excellent that it was all the more interesting and invigorating when he could go away for a time and be a companion to someone else, to Willie Shaftoe, for instance, with whom he sometimes stayed in his place near Carlisle, or even for a few days' golf with the Reverend Thomas Bird, rector of a church in Keswick.

Mrs Penwin in fact had nerves quite in spite of his profound devotion to her, never entirely captured the whole of her husband—a small fragment eternally escaped her, and this escape was a very real grievance to her. Like a wise woman she did not make scenes—no English husband can endure scenes—but she was always attempting to stop up this one little avenue of escape. But most provoking! So soon as one avenue was closed another would appear.

She realized very quickly (for she was not at all a fool) that this Alsatian was assisting her husband to escape from her because his presence in their household was bringing him into closer contact with Blake. Both the Penwins feared Blake and admired him; to friends and strangers they spoke of him with intense pride. "What we should do without Blake I can't think!" "But aren't we lucky in *these* days to have a chauffeur whom we can completely trust?"

Nevertheless, behind these sentiments there was this great difference, that Mrs. Penwin disliked Blake extremely (whenever he looked at her he made her feel a weak, helpless, and idiotic woman) while Charlie Penwin, although he was afraid of him, in his heart liked him very much indeed.

If Blake only were human, little Charlie Penwin, who was a sentimentalist, used to think—and now suddenly Blake *was* human. He had gone "dotty" about this dog, and the dog followed him like a shadow. So close were they the one to the other that you could almost imagine that they held conversations together.

Then Blake came into his master's room one day to ask whether Adam could sleep in his room. He had a small room next to Mrs. Blake's because he was often out late with the car at night or must rise very early in the morning. Clara Blake liked to have her sleep undisturbed.

"You see, sir," he said, "he won't sort of settle down in the outhouse. He's restless. I know he is."

"How do you know he is?" asked Charlie Penwin.

"I can sort of feel it, sir. He won't be no sort of trouble in my room, and he'll be a fine guard to the house at night."

The two men looked at one another and were in that moment friends. They both smiled.

"Very well, Blake. I don't think there's anything against it."

Of course, there *were* things against it. Mrs. Penwin hated the idea of the dog sleeping in the house. She did not really hate it; what she hated was that Blake and her husband should settle this thing without a word to her. Nor, when she protested would her husband falter. Blake wanted it. It would be a good protection for the house.

Blake developed a very odd whistle with which he called the dog. Putting his fingers into his mouth he called forth this strange melancholy note that seemed to penetrate into endless distance and that had in it something mysterious, melancholy, and dangerous. It was musical and inhuman; friends of the Penwins, comfortably at tea, would hear this thin whistling cry, coming, it seemed, from far away beyond the fells, having in it some part of the lake and the distant sea trembling on Drigg sands and of the lonely places in Eskdale and Ennerdale.

"What's that?" they would say, looking up.

"Oh, it's Blake calling the dog."

"What a strange whistle!"

"Yes, it's the only one the dog hears."

The dog did hear it, at any distance, in any place. When Blake went with the car the Alsatian would lie on the upper lawn whence he could see the road and wait for his return.

He would both see and hear the car's return, but he would not stir until Blake, released from his official duties, could whistle to him—then with one bound he would be up, down the garden, and with his front paws up against Blake's chest would show him his joy.

To all the rest of the world he was indifferent. But he was not hostile. He showed indeed an immense patience, and especially with regard to the Sealyham.

The dog Mopsa attempted twice at least every day to kill the Alsatian. He succeeded in biting him severely but so long as Blake was there he showed an infinite control, letting Blake part them although every instinct in him was stirred to battle.

But after a time, Blake became clever at keeping the two dogs separate; moreover, the Sealyham became afraid of Blake. He was clever enough to realize that when he fought the Alsatian he fought Blake as well—and Blake was too much for him.

Very soon however, Blake was at war not only with the Sealyham but with his wife and Mrs. Penwin too. You might think that the works "at war" were too strong when nothing was to be seen on the surface. Mrs. Blake said nothing, Mrs. Penwin said nothing, Blake himself said nothing.

Save for the fights with the Sealyham, there was no charge whatever to bring against the Alsatian. He was never in anyone's way, he brought no dirt in the house; whenever Charlie Penwin took him in the car he sat motionless on the back seat, his wolf ears pricked up, his large and beautiful eyes sternly regarding the outside world, but his consciousness fixed only upon Blake's back, broad and masterly above the wheel.

No charge could be brought against him except that the devotion between the man and the dog was in this little house of ordered emotions, routine habits, quiet sterility almost terrible. Mrs. Blake, as her husband left her one night to return to his own room, broke out: "If you'd loved me as you love that dog I'd have had a different life."

Blake patted her shoulder, moist beneath her nightdress. "I love you all right, my girl," he said.

And Mrs Penwin found that here she could not move her husband. Again and again she said: "Charlie, that dog's got to go."

"Why?"

"It's dangerous."

"I don't see it."

"Somebody will be bitten one day, and then you *will* see it."

"There's a terrible lot of nonsense talked about Alsatians—"

And then, when everyone was comfortable, Mrs. Blake reading her "Home Chat," Mrs Penwin her novel, Mrs. Fern (Mrs. Penwin's best friend) doing a "cross-word," over the misty, dank garden, carried it seemed by the muffled clouds that floated above the fell, would sound that strange melancholy whistle, so distant and yet so near, Blake calling his dog.

For Blake himself life was suddenly, and for the first time, complete. He had not known, all this while, what it was that he missed although he had known that he missed something. Had Mrs. Blake given him a child he would have realized completion. Mrs. Blake alone had not been enough for his heart. In this dog he found fulfillment because here were all the things that he admired—loyalty, strength, courage, self-reliance, fidelity, comradeship, and, above all, sobriety of speech and behavior. Beyond these there was something more—love. He did not, even to himself, admit the significance of this yet deeper contact. And he analyzed nothing.

For the dog, life in this dangerous menacing country of the enemy was at last secure and simple. He had only one thing to do, only one person to consider.

But, of course, life is not so simple as this for anybody. A battle was being waged, and it must have an issue.

The Penwins were not in Cumberland during the winter. They went to their little place in Sussex, very close to London and to all their London friends. Mrs. Penwin would not take the Alsatian to Sussex. "But why not?" asked Charlie. She hated it, Mrs. Blake hated it. That, Charlie objected, was not reason enough.

"Do you realize," said Mrs. Penwin theatrically, "that this dog is dividing us?"

"Nonsense," said Charlie.

"It is not nonsense. I believe you care more for Blake than you do for me." She cried. She cried very seldom. Charlie Penwin was uncomfortable but some deep male obstinacy was roused in him. This had become an affair of the sexes. Men must stand together and protect themselves or they would be swept away in this feminine flood.

Blake knew, Mrs. Blake knew, Mrs. Penwin knew that the dog would go with them to Sussex unless some difinite catastrophe gave Mrs. Penwin the victory.

Lying on his bed at night, seeing the gray wolf-like shadow of the dog stretched on the floor, Blacke's soul for the first time in its history trembled, at the thought of the slight movement, incident, spoken word, sound that might rouse the dog beyond his endurance and precipitate the catastrophe. The dog was behaving magnificently, but he was surrounded by his enemies. Did he know what hung upon his restraint?

Whether he knew or no, the catastrophe arrived and arrived with the utmost, most violent publicity. On a sun-gleaming, russet October afternoon, on the lawn while Charlie was giving Blake instructions about the car and Mrs. Penwin put in also her word, Mopsa attacked the Alsatian. Blake ran to separate them, and the Alsatian sharply bitten, bewildered, humiliated, snapped and caught Blake's leg between his teeth. A moment later he and Blake knew, both of them, what he had done. Blake would have hidden it, but blood was flowing. In the Alsatian's heart remorse, terror, love, and a sense of disaster—a confirmation of all that, since his birth, knowing the traps that his enemies would lay for him, he has suspected—leapt to life together.

Disregarding all else, he looked up at Blake.

"And that settles it!" cried Mrs. Penwin, triumphantly. "He goes!"

Blake's leg was badly bitten in three places; there would be scars for life. And it was settled. Before the week was out the dog would be returned to his first owners, who did not want him—who would give him to someone else who also, in turn, through fear or shyness of neighbors, would not want him.

Two days after this catastrophe, Mrs. Blake went herself to Mrs. Penwin.

"My husband's that upset—I wouldn't care if the stays, Mum."

"Why, Clara, you hate the dog."

"Oh well, Mum, Blake's a good husband to me. I don't like to see him—"

"Why, what has he said?"

"He hasn't said *anything*, Mum."

But Mrs. Penwin shook her head. "No, Clara, it's ridiculous. The dog's dangerous."

And Blake went to Charlie Penwin. The two men faced one another and were closer together, fonder of one another, man caring for man, than they had ever been before.

"But, Blake, if the dog bites *you* whom he cares for—I mean, don't you see? He really *is* dangerous—"

"He wasn't after biting me," said Blake slowly. "And if he *had* to bite somebody, being aggravated and nervous, he'd not find anyone better to bite than me who understands him and knows he don't mean nothing by it."

Charlie Penwin felt in himself a terrible disloyalty to his wife. She could go to— Why should not Blake have his dog? Was he forever to be dominated by women? For a brief rocking, threatening moment his whole ordered world trembled. He knew that if he said the dog was to remain the dog would remain and that something would have broken between his wife and himself that could never be mended.

He looked at Blake, who with his blue serious eyes stared steadily in front of him. He hesistated. He shook his head.

"No, Blake, it won't do. Mrs. Penwin will never be easy now while the dog is here."

Later in the day Blake did an amazing thing. He went to Mrs. Penwin.

During all these years he had never voluntarily, himself, gone to Mrs. Penwin. He had never gone unless he was sent for. She looked at him and felt, as she always did, dislike, admiration, and herself a bit of a fool.

"Well, Blake?"

"If the dog stays I'll make myself responsible. He shan't bite nobody again."

"But how can you tell? You said he wouldn't bite anyone before and he did."

"He won't again."

"No, Blake, he's got to go. I shan't have a moment's peace while he's here."

"He's a wonderful dog. I'll have him trained so he won't hurt a fly. He's like a child with me."

"I'm sure he is. Irresponsible like a child. That's why he bit you."

"I don't make nothing of his biting me."

"You may not, but next time it will be someone else. There's something in the paper about them every day."

"He's like a child with me."

"I'm very sorry, Blake. I can't give way about it. You'll see I'm right in the end. My husband ought never to have accepted the dog at all."

After Blake had gone she did not know why, but she felt uneasy, as though she had robbed a blind man, or stolen another woman's lover. Ridiculous! There could be no question but that she was right.

Blake admitted that to himself. She was right. He did not criticise her, but he did not know what to do. He had never felt like this in all his life before as though part of himself were being torn from him.

On the day before the dog was to go back to his original owners Blake was sent into Keswick to make some purchases. It was a soft blooming day, one of those North English autumn days when there is a scent of spices in the sharp air and a rosy light hangs about the trees. Blake had taken the dog with him, and driving back along the lake, seeing how it lay, a sheet of silver glass upon whose surface the islands were painted in flat colors of auburn and smoky gray, a sudden madness seized him. It was the stillness, the silence, the breathless pause—

Instead of turning to the right over the Grange bridge, he drove the car straight on into Borrowdale. It was yet early in the afternoon—all the lovely valley lay in gold leaf at the feet of the russet hills, and no cloud moved in the sky. He took the car to Seatoller and climbed with the dog the steep path toward Honister.

And the dog thought that at last what he had longed for was to come to pass. He and Blake were at length free, they would go on and on, leaving all the stupid, nerve-jumping world behind them, never to return to it.

With a wild, fierce happiness such as he had never yet shown he bounded forward, drinking in the cold streams, feeling the strong turf beneath his feet, running back to Blake to assure him of his comradeship. At last he was free, and life was noble as it ought to be.

At the turn of the road Blake sat down and looked back. All around him were hills. Nothing moved; only the stream close to him slipped murmuring between the boulders. The hills ran from horizon to horizon, and between gray clouds a silver strip of sky, lit by an invisible sun, ran like a river into mist. Blake called the dog to him and laid his hand upon his head. He knew that the dog thought that they both had escaped forever now from the world. Well, why not? They could walk on, on to the foot of the hill on whose skyline the mining hut stood like a

listening ear, down the Pass to Buttermere, past the lake, past Crummock Water to Cockermouth. There would be a train. It would not be difficult for him to get work. His knowledge of cars (he had a genius for them) would serve him anywhere. And Clara? She was almost invisible, a tiny what blot on the horizon. She would find someone else. His hand tightened about the dog's head.

For a long while he sat there, the dog never moving, the silver river spreading in the sky, the hills gathering closer about him.

Suddenly he shook his head. No, he could not. He would be running away, a poor kind of cowardice. He pulled Adam's sharp ears; he buried his face in Adam's fur. He stood up, and Adam also stood up, placed his paws on Blake's chest, licked his cheeks. In his eyes there shone great happiness because they two were going alone together.

But Blake turned back down the path, and the dog realizing that there was to be no freedom, walked close behind him, brushing with his body sometimes the stuff of Blake's trousers.

Next day Blake took the dog back to the place whence he had come.

Two days later, the dog, knowing that he was not wanted, sat watching a little girl who played some foolish game near him. She had plump bare legs; he watched them angrily. He was unhappy, lonely, nervous, once more in the land of the enemy, and now with no friend.

Through the air, mingling with the silly laughter of the child and other dangerous sounds came, he thought, a whistle. His heart hammered. His ears were up. With all his strength he bounded towards the sound. But he was chained. To-morrow he was to be given to a Cumberland farmer.

Mrs. Penwin was entertaining two ladies at tea. This was the last day before the journey south. Across the dank lawns came that irritating, melancholy whistle disturbing her, reproaching her— and for what?

Why, for her sudden suspicion that everything in life was just ajar—one little push and all would be in its place—but would she be married to Charlie, would Mrs. Plang then be jealous of her pretty daughter, would Miss Tennyson, nibbling now at her pink pieces of icing, be nursing her aged and intemperate father? She looked up crossly.

"Really, Charlie, that must be Blake whistling. I can't think why now the dog's gone. To let us know what he thinks about it, I suppose." She turned to her friends, "Our chauffeur—a splendid man—we *are* so fortunate. Charlie, do tell him. It's such a hideous whistle, anyway—and now the dog is gone—"

John Steinbeck

1902-1968

TRAVELS
WITH CHARLEY

There was some genuine worry about my traveling alone, open to attack, robbery, assault. It is well known that our roads are dangerous. And here I admit I had senseless qualms. It is some years since I have been alone, nameless, friendless, without any of the safety one gets from family, friends, and accomplices. There is no reality in the danger. It's just a very lonely, helpless feeling at first—a kind of desolate feeling. For this reason I took one companion on my journey—an old French gentleman poodle known as Charley. Actually his name is Charles le Chien. He was born in Bercy on the outskirts of Paris and trained in France, and while he knows a little poodle-English, he responds quickly only to commands in French. Otherwise he has to translate, and that slows him down. He is a very big poodle, of a color called *bleu*, and he is blue when he is clean. Charley is a born diplomat. He prefers negotiation to fighting, and properly so, since he is very bad at fighting. Only once in his ten years has he been in trouble—when he met a dog who refused to negotiate. Charley lost a piece of his right ear that time. But he is a good watch dog—has a roar like a lion, designed to conceal from night-wandering strangers the fact that he couldn't bite his way out of a *cornet du papier*. He is a good friend and traveling companion, and would rather travel about than anything he can imagine. If he occurs at length in this account, it is because he contributed much to the trip. A dog, particularly an exotic like Charley, is a bond between strangers. Many conversations en route began with "What degree of a dog is that?"

Charley is a tall dog. As he sat in the seat beside me, his head was almost as high as mine. He put his nose close to my ear and said, "Ftt." He is the only dog I ever knew who could pronounce the consonant *F*. This is because his front teeth are crooked, a tragedy which keeps him out of dog shows; because his upper front teeth slightly engage his lower lip Charley can pronounce *F*. The word "Ftt" usually means he would like to salute a bush or a tree. I opened the cab door and let him out, and he went about his ceremony. He doesn't have to think about it to do it well. It is my experience that in some areas Charley is more intelligent than I am, but in others he is abysmally ignorant. He can't read, can't drive a car, and has no grasp of mathematics. But in his own field of endeavor, which he was now practicing, the slow, imperial smelling over and anointing of an area, he has no peer. Of course his horizons are limited, but how wide are mine?

Charley likes to get up early, and he likes me to get up early too. And why shouldn't he? Right after his breakfast he goes back to sleep. Over the years he has developed a number of innocent-appearing ways to get me up. He can shake himself and his collar loud enough to wake the dead. If that doesn't work he gets a sneezing fit. But perhaps his most irritating method is to sit quietly beside the bed and stare into my face with a sweet and forgiving look on his face; I come out of deep sleep with the feeling of being looked at. But I have learned to keep my eyes tight shut. If I even blink he sneezed and stretches, and that night's sleep is over for me. Often the war of wills goes on for quite a time, I squinching my eyes shut and he forgiving me, but he nearly always wins. He liked traveling so much he wanted to get started early, and early for Charley is the first tempering of darkness with the dawn.

I must confess to a laxness in the matter of National Parks. I haven't visited many of them. Perhaps this is because they enclose the unique, the spectacular, the astounding—the greatest waterfall, the deepest canyon, the highest cliff, the most stupendous works of man or nature. And I would rather see a good Brady photograph than Mount Rushmore. For it is my opinion that we enclose and celebrate the freaks of our nation and of our civilization. Yellowstone National Park is no more representative of America than is Disneyland.

This being my natural attitude, I don't know what made me turn sharply south and cross a state line to take a look at Yellowstone. Perhaps it was a fear of my neighbors. I could hear them say, "You mean you were that near to Yellowstone and didn't go? You must be crazy." Again it might have been the American tendency in travel. One goes, not so much to see but to tell afterward. Whatever my purpose in going to Yellowstone, I'm glad I went because I discovered something about Charley I might never have known.

A pleasant-looking National Park man checked me in and then he said, "How about that dog? They aren't permitted in except on leash."

"Why?" I asked.

"Because of the bears."

"Sir," I said, "this is an unique dog. He does not live by tooth or fang. He respects the right of cats to be cats although he doesn't admire them. He turns his steps rather than disturb an earnest caterpillar. His greatest fear is that someone will point out a

95

rabbit and suggest that he chase it. This is a dog of peace and tranquility. I suggest that the greatest danger to your bears will be pique at being ignored by Charley."

The young man laughed. "I wasn't so much worried about the bears," he said. "But our bears have developed an intolerance for dogs. One of them might demonstrate his prejudice with a clip on the chin, and then—no dog."

"I'll lock him in the back, sir. I promise you Charley will cause no ripple in the bear world, and as an old bear-looker, neither will I."

"I just have to warn you," he said. "I have no doubt your dog has the best of intentions. On the other hand, our bears have the worst. Don't leave food about. Not only do they steal but they are critical of anyone who tries to reform them. In a word, don't believe their sweet faces or you might get clobbered. And don't let the dog wander. Bears don't argue."

We went on our way into the wonderland of nature gone nuts, and you will have to believe what happened. The only way I can prove it would be to get a bear.

Less than a mile from the entrance I saw a bear beside the road, and it ambled out as though to flag me down. Instantly a change came over Charley. He shrieked with rage. His lips flared, showing wicked teeth that have some trouble with a dog biscuit. He screeched insults at the bear, which hearing, the bear reared up and seemed to me to overtop Rocinante. Frantically I rolled the windows shut and, swinging quickly to the left, grazed the animal, then scuttled on while Charley raved and ranted beside me, describing in detail what he would do to that bear if he could get at him. I was never so astonished in my life. To the best of my knowledge Charley had never seen a bear, and in his whole history had showed great tolerance for every living thing. Besides all this, Charley is a coward, so deep-seated a coward that he has developed a technique for concealing it. And yet he showed every evidence of wanting to get out and murder a bear that outweighed him a thousand to one. I don't understand it.

A little farther along two bears showed up, and the effect was doubled. Charley became a maniac. He leaped all over me, he cursed and growled, snarled and screamed. I didn't know he had the ability to snarl. Where did he learn it? Bears were in good supply, and the road became a nightmare. For the first time in his life Charley resisted reason, even resisted a cuff on the ear. He became a primitive killer lusting for the blood of his enemy, and up to this moment he had had no enemies. In a bearless stretch, I opened the cab, took Charley by the

collar, and locked him in the house. But that did no good. When we passed other bears he leaped on the table and scratched at the windows trying to get out at them. I could hear canned goods crashing as he struggled in his mania. Bears simply brought out the Hyde in my Jekyll-headed dog. What could have caused it? Was it a pre-breed memory of a time when the wolf was in him? I know him well. Once in a while he tries a bluff, but it is a palpable lie. I swear that this was no lie. I am certain that if he were released he would have charged every bear we passed and found victory or death.

It was too nerve-wracking, a shocking spectacle, like seeing an old, calm friend go insane. No amount of natural wonders, of rigid cliffs and belching waters, of smoking springs could even engage my attention while that pandemonium went on. After about the fifth encounter I gave up, turned Rocinante about, and retraced my way. If I had stopped the night and bears had gathered to my cooking, I dare not think what would have happened.

At the gate the park guard checked me out. "You didn't stay long. Where's the dog?"

"Locked up back there. And I owe you an apology. That dog has the heart and soul of a bear-killer and I didn't know it. Heretofore he has been a little tender-hearted toward an underdone steak."

"Yeah!" he said. "That happens sometimes. That's why I warned you. A bear dog would know his chances, but I've seen a Pomeranian go up like a puff of smoke. You know, a well-favored bear can bat a dog like a tennis ball."

I moved fast, back the way I had come, and I was reluctant to camp for fear there might be some unofficial non-government bears about. That night I spent in a pretty auto court near Livingston. I had my dinner in a restaurant, and when I had settled in with a drink and a comfortable chair and my bathed bare feet on a carpet with red roses, I inspected Charley. He was dazed. His eyes held a faraway look and he was totally exhausted, emotionally no doubt. Mostly he reminded me of a man coming out of a long, hard drunk—worn out, depleted, collapsed. He couldn't eat his dinner, he refused the evening walk, and once we were in he collapsed on the floor and went to sleep. In the night I heard him whining and yapping, and when I turned on the light his feet were making running gestures and his body jerked and his eyes were wide open, but it was only a night bear. I awakened him and gave him some water. This time he went to sleep and didn't stir all night. In the morning he was still tired. I wonder why we think the thoughts and emotions of animals are simple.

Ring Lardner

1885-1933

DOGS

Every little wile you hear people talking about a man that they don't nobody seem to have much use for him on acct. of him not paying his debts or beating his wife or something and everybody takes a rap at him about this and that until finely one of the party speaks up and says they must be some good in him because he likes animals.

"A man can't be all bad when he is so kind to dogs." That is what they generally always say and that is the reason you see so many men stop on the st. when they see a dog and pet it because they figure that may be somebody will be looking at them do it, and the next time they are getting panned, why whoever seen it will speak up and say:

"He can't be all bad because he likes dogs."

Well friends when you come right down to cases they's about as much sence to this as a good many other delusions that we got here in this country, like for inst. the one about nobody wanting to win the first pot and the one about the whole lot of authors not being able to do their best work unlest they are ½ pickled.

Pretty near everybody wants to be well thought of and if liking dogs or sheep is helping along these lines, why even if I don't like them, I wouldn't never loose a opportunity to be seen in their company and act as if I was haveing the time of my life.

But wile I was raised in a kennel, you might say, and some of my most intimate childhood friends

was of the canine gender, still in all I believe dogs is better in some climates than others, the same as oysters, and I don't think it should ought to be held against a man if he don't feel the same towards N.Y. dogs as he felt towards Michigan dogs, and I am free to confess that the 4 dogs who I have grew to know personly here on Long Island has failed to arouse tender yearnings anyways near similar to those inspired by the flea bearers of my youth.

And in case they should be any tendency on the part of my readers to denounce me for failing to respond whole heartily to the wiles of the Long Island breed let me present a brief sketch of some so as true lovers of the canine tribe can judge for themselfs if the fault is all mine.

NO. I

This was the dainty boy that belonged to Gene Buck and it was a bull dog no bigger than a 2 car garage and it wouldn't harm a hair of nobody's head only other animals and people. Children were as safe with this pet as walking in the Pittsburgh freight yards and he wouldn't think of no more wronging a cat than scratching himself.

In fairness to Mr. Buck I'll state that a pal of his give him the dog as a present without no comment. Well they wasn't no trouble till Gene had the dog pretty near ½ hour when they let him out. He was gone 10 minutes during which Gene received a couple of phone calls announcing more in anger than in sorrow the sudden deaths of 2 adjacent cats of noble berth so when the dog come back Gene spanked him and after that he didn't kill no more cats except when he got outdoors.

But the next day De Wolf Hopper come over to call and brought his kid which the dog thought would look better with one leg and it took 5 people to get him not to operate, so after that Gene called up the supt. of a dogs reform school and the man said he would take him and cure him of the cat habit by tying one of his victims around his neck and leaving it there for a wk. but he didn't know how to cure the taste for young Hoppers unlest De Wolf could spare the kid the wk. after they was finished with the cat.

NO. 2

The people that lived 3 houses from the undersigned decided to move to England where it seems like you can't take dogs no more so they asked us did we want the dog as it was very nice around children and we took it and sure enough it was OK in regards to children but it shared this new owners feeling towards motorcycles and every time one went past the house the dog would run out and spill the contents, and on Sundays when the traffic was heavy they would sometimes be as many as 4 to 5 motorcycle jehus standing on their heads in the middle of the road.

One of them finely took offence and told on the dog and the justice of the peace called me up and said I would have to kill it within 24 hrs. and the only way I could think of to do same was drown it in the bath tub and if you done that, why the bath tub wouldn't be no good no more because it was a good sized dog and no matter how often you pulled the stopper it would still be there.

The next-door neighbors has a pro-German police dog that win a blue ribbon once but now it acts as body guard for the lady of the house and one day we was over there and the host says to slap his Mrs. on the arm and see what happened so I slapped her on the arm and I can still show you what happened.

When you dance with mine hostess this sweet little pet dances right along with you and watches your step and if you tred on my ladys toe he fines you a mouth full and if you and her is partners in a bridge game he lays under the table and you either bid right and play right or you get nipped.

NO. 4

This is our present incumbrance which we didn't ask for him and nobody give him to us but here he is and he has got the insomnia and he has picked a spot outside my window to enjoy it but not only that but he has learnt that if you jump at a screen often enough it will finely give way and the result is that they ain't a door or window on the first floor that you couldn't drive a rhinoceros through it and all the bugs that didn't already live in the house is moveing in and bringing their family.

That is a true record of the dogs who I have met since takeing up my abode in Nassau county so when people ask me do I like dogs I say I'm crazy about them and I think they are all right in their place but it ain't Long Island.

Frank Debenham

1883-1965

**STAREEK,
A SLEDGE DOG WITH
SCOTT IN THE
ANTARCTIC**

Every expedition which has employed dog transport will testify to the valiant work performed by their teams and will be ready with stories about their more notable dogs. They will tell of dog heroes who pulled a taut trace to their last breath, of dogs who lost heart early in the journey, of shy dogs and bold dogs, of those who were popular with the whole team and others against whom every fang was turned. Dog personality is, in fact, one of the first things a driver learns and the better he learns it the better driver he will be.

Amongst the dogs of any expedition there will always be one or two who in character and performance have towered above their fellows, and with whom their drivers would willingly share their honours...

Of the forty-five dogs taken by Captain Scott on his last expedition (1910-13) all but two were from Eastern Siberia, where they had been post dogs, carrying the mail in winter where no other transport could pass. Though varied in colour and in size as is the way with sledge dogs, they were on the whole of a stockier build than the Canadian or West Greenland breed, whose longer legs might well carry them faster but hardly farther than their cousins of Eastern Asia. They were not much given to howling in concert nor to great enmity amongst themselves, so that compared to some other expeditions we had fairly quiet nights, and mass-murders, when a very unpopular dog was killed by the rest for no reason that we could discover, were very rare occurrences.

The only time that they were really noisy was when a man came out of the hut with a dog harness over his arm and the whole of the dog lines would leap forward as one dog with full-throated demand to be selected. The few dogs who could be trusted off the chain would race up and these would try to wriggle their heads through the dangling loops of the harness. For the most part a sledge dog has a happy life and he enjoys most of his sledge hauling just as much as the house dog loves his daily walk round the park or the shepherd's dog his disciplined labour with the flock. Nor does he really suffer badly from the weather except when he is forced to travel into a strong wind. He finds a blizzard monotonous, but snuggling under the snow which soon covers his coat he is warm enough; indeed the only

type of weather which thoroughly annoys him is a temperature above freezing point with its accompanying wet, and in the Antarctic he is spared that.

Even on the voyage down the men soon began to learn the names and the characters of the dogs and to choose those they preferred for one characteristic or another. Captain Scott alone did not voice his preference, but we always suspected that his favourite was Osman, a large black dog who was reputed to be king-dog, that is to say, acknowledged as the most redoubtable fighter. Tough and enduring he proved to be and on one occasion he held up half the weight of ten dogs dangling in their harnesses down a crevass, the men hanging on to the sledge on one side and Osman on the other, and it was at least five minutes before the strain could be taken off his trace. On this occasion two of the dogs struggled free of their harness and fell on to a block of hard snow 65 feet below the surface, and when Scott reached them an hour later at the end of a rope they had curled up and gone to sleep.

Rather more friendly was Lappa ('flop-eared'), who was the inseparable companion of Osman and backed up his sinewy strength with canine intellect.

Demitri, the Siberian dog-boy, seemed to favour the burly but rather dour Volk, who he always insisted was the 'strongest of all the dogs.'

As each dog had his individual character one had a wide choice, and each in turn had his individual adventures, sometimes fatal. One of the more beautiful, Vaida, was described by Scott as 'especially distinguished for his savage temper and generally uncouth manners' on the first journey. But he improved with friendly treatment and three months later earned the note 'he now allows me to rub him and push him about without the slightest protest. He is a strange beast—I imagine so unused to kindness that it took him time to appreciate it.'

Their characters showed up in all kinds of amusing ways, as is evident from a note in Wilson's diary. 'I have a funny little dog, Mukaka, small but very game and a good worker. He is paired with a fat, lazy and very greedy black dog, Nugis by name, and on every march this sprightly little Mukaka will once or twice notice that Nugis is not pulling and will jump over the trace, bite Nugis like a snap, and be back again in his own place before the fat dog knows what has happened.'

Only a small part of their individual adventures is known. Mukaka ('monkey'), for instance, turned back from a journey for some reason to a deserted hut where I found him a month later, and Julik ('Scamp') was away for a month in the depth of winter, having probably floated away on an ice floe, but turned up in due course and lived to pull his part

on the Pole journey.

Amongst these and many more interesting dog personalities Stareek stood out, not so much for his temperament, which was quiet, but for his air of wisdom and his leadership at the head of a team. He was older than most of his companions and had been a trapper's dog on the great Amur river before he took to the mail sledge. Perhaps this more varied life had helped to give him his appearance of vast experience and calm judgment, but his name means 'Old Man' and more probably he was born with that look of solemn wisdom and was therefore so christened by his owner.

In the South his first driver was Dr Edward Wilson, and some extracts from Wilson's diaries and letters will serve as introduction better than words of mine.

'I have a delightful leader, "Stareek" by name —Russian for "Old Man," and he is the most wise old man.'.... 'He is quite the nicest, quietest, cleverest old dog I have ever come across. He looks in fact as though he knew all the wickedness of all the world and all its cares, and as if he were bored to death by them.'...'Even now, six months after I have had anything to do with him, he never fails to come and speak to me whenever he sees me.'

It was not everyone who took to Stareek and there were those who said that his slightly tip-tilted nose betokened disdain or misanthropy, that his slow walk with a slight limp when he first uncurled himself from rest was malingering, and so on. He was not one to curry favour by extravagant tail-waggings or to go berserk with blood-lust at sight of penguins. He rather kept himself to himself and made no advances to man or dog. If you wanted to make friends with him you had to go more than half-way yourself. After his great adventure it fell to me to have him as my leader, but even without that feat behind him I should have done my best to get behind his barrier of restraint, and in the end I did.

In the first season of depot-laying journeys Stareek was the most reliable of the leaders and, as we have seen, won great praise and affection from Dr Wilson. He was able to meet unexpected mishaps with greater resource and rarely seemed surprised at any new phenomenon. Even the apparently alarming noise of the escaping air when an area of packed snow sank suddenly under the weight of the sledge did not produce panic in him as it did in most of the dogs. Wilson described his reaction this way.

'There were innumerable subsidences of the surface—the breaking of crusts over air spaces with a hushing sort of noise or muffled report. My leader Stareek thought there was a rabbit under the crust every time one gave way close by him and he would jump sideways with both feet on the spot and his nose in the snow. The action was like a flash and never checked the team.' The 'Barrier Hush,' as it came to be called, later became a source of interest to all the dogs and was welcomed by the drivers for that reason.

The general opinion of Stareek at this time is voiced by Scott in a note written towards the end of the depot journey, when different leaders had been tried in the other team. 'Osman is restored to leadership today: it is curious how these leaders come on and go off, all except old Stareek, who remains as steady as ever.'

With such a reputation it was clear that he would be one of the leaders for the two teams who were to accompany the Southern Parties next year. He came through the winter very well, probably because of his intelligence. But he was getting old, and I remember Meares, who was in command of the dog teams, saying that he wished he could devise a way by which Stareek could lead without using up his strength in pulling. It was his influence on the team as a whole which was so valuable, particularly in the conditions of Barrier travel.

Scott was much interested in the dogs and there are many notes about them in his diary, many of them about the effect of the Barrier on the dogs: 'A dog must be either eating, asleep, or interested. His eagerness to snatch at interest, to chain his attention to something, is almost pathetic! The monotony of marching kills him. This is the fearfullest difficulty for the dog driver on a snow plain without leading marks or objects in sight. The dog is almost human in its demand for living interest, yet fatally less than human in its inability to forsee. A dog lives for the day, the hour, even the moment. The human being can live and support discomfort for the future.' It may well be that Stareek's greater intelligence, or some mental power through which he was not so dependent on external interests, was the secret both of his influence on his team and his resistance to the Barrier *ennui* which attacked the other dogs.

But mental resources could not entirely make up for the failing sinews of age, and when the teams had done some 300 miles of the journey Polewards it was clear that Stareek was near the end of his tether. From this point two men, Day and Hooper, were to return, manhauling their sledge, and Scott decided to send back, under their care, the two dogs which were failing fast, Stareek and Czigane. Though there was no dog food to be spared for them there was a sporting chance that with odd scraps from the men they might get back to the base and live to pull another day. Cizgane strongly approved of this turn in his affairs and trotted along beside the men as the turned

northwards. Stareek, on the other hand, strongly resented either his deposition or his separation and refused to go. He had to be tied to the sledge and spent most of the first day actively resisting by pulling the wrong way, or escaping and having to be retrieved by chase. By the end of the day two rather exasperated men made up their minds that they would not repeat the performance and Stareek would have to decide for himself. He made the decision during the night by gnawing through his lashing and his tracks showed in the morning that he had gone back to his team. The two men wondered how long it would take him to catch them up and how soon he would have to be killed and fed to his own team: for them that was the end of Stareek.

But he never caught up with the Southern Parties, perhaps because he found they were too far ahead, perhaps some dog-reasoning told him that after all northward was his best course, and that since loyalty was denied him self-preservation should rank first.

Meanwhile the two men hauled their sledge a regular ten or twelve miles a day with Czigane walking beside them and faring pretty well as far as comfort was concerned; a bed of soft material was made up for him on the sledge each night, and the men went short on biscuit to keep their companion strong enough to get along. They never guessed that somewhere behind on that featureless barren plain a much older dog was doing his best to catch them up, or could they have done anything had they guessed, since they had to keep up the average pace their ration of provisions prescribed for them.

On the eighteenth night, when they had gone some 200 miles since seeing the last of Stareek, the man camped, now in sight of land though still 100 miles from home. They tucked Czigane up as usual, but their night was much disturbed by Czigane barking instead of sleeping quietly as was his wont, so that the men thought that a wandering skua, 100 miles from the sea, must be flying around.

When in the morning they opened the tent door they say the cause of Czigane's complaining barks, for he was lying on the less comfortable snow and on the sledge was—Stareek. Or perhaps one should say, the shadow of Stareek, for he was so weak and emaciated that he could not stand up or make more than the feeblest sign of greeting. In almost any other country Stareek, as he reached each camp site, would have been able to sniff round and pick up some small trifle of waste, but not on the Barrier, where not a scrap of nourishment, even of the most nauseating kind, was ever left. Even the excrement of pony, man and dog was cleaned up by the dogs, there was nothing left. It must have been with literally his last ounce of energy—or was it mental grit—that he had staggered into camp in the night and, with the leader's authority still within him, had ordered Czigane off the bed on the sledge. Naturally the men could hardly believe it possible, and they feared that he might have broken into one of the depots of food for the returning parties. This would have been a big task for a weak dog and it was in fact found later that he did not even attempt the task of scraping down piles of snow blocks.

Filled with admiration for such a feat of endurance they pulled him on the sledge for a couple of marches, fed him cautiously and to their great pride he finished the last lap home on his own feet, still very weak but saved.

At first sight one is tempted to sum up this astonishing journey as yet another instance of the endurance of sledge dogs which is always surprising us, and of an instinct which is beyond our comprehension.

Yet that would be a very inadequate explanation, for many other dogs have failed to rejoin their party under similar or easier circumstances. That same summer, only a few hundred miles to the east on the same Barrier, Amundsen lost several dogs who for one reason or other left the teams and never returned. It seems that usually such a 'lost' dog either wanders off the track, presumably in search of food, and fails to find it again, or, reaching one of the camps he has visited before, he stays their till he dies, hoping that the men will come back.

Stareek's behaviour therefore at once marks an unusual intelligence, but still more that mental persistance, that refusal to give in which we now express by the word 'gut'. None but a dog of strong character would have continued day after day in his 200-mile pursuit when the simpler way would have been to lie down in the snow and forget his pains in a sleep unto death as many another had done before him.

One wonders whether, as he reached each camp site of the men, his sense of smell gave him some indication that he was catching up. Beyond that encouragement there could have been nothing but his indomitable will and his unusual brain to spur him on to yet another and another day of forcing his tired body on. It seems probable that at the end he must have been only a little way behind them for several days, because while he was fairly fresh his pace would have been faster than that of men pulling a sledge, whereas later he must have been hard put to it to travel ten miles or so in the day.

Whatever details of his journey, which must remain mere guesswork, it is clear that only mental strength could have carried him over the last stages; it was a victory of the spirit even more than of muscle.

Back at the base Stareek's recovery was slow but steady, and when I returned some two months later I could at first see very little difference. There was a difference, however, as well there might be, and it took the form of a greater inclination for men's society and less for that of the dogs. He was never unpopular with the other dogs, but he now kept apart from all their mass reactions, and seemed to regard them all as careless adolescents. Nor did he like petting unless it took the form of brushing his coat free from ice; he would move away if you merely patted him for patting's sake. He liked the presence of his men friends but did not want their fussy attentions.

As the light came back with the next spring he would accompany me on my walks, but he would not go far and he would often lie down on a rise, keeping me withing sight, and rejoin me as I returned without showing any signs of greeting or affection but merely a certain mild satisfaction in my presence.

Naturally I was very pleased when he was allotted to me as the leader for a team of dogs given to me for short geological journeys near the base. He took no interest whatever in them as a team, probably because it was composed of all the left-overs and misfits from the two 'professional' teams, yet there was no doubt about his authority over them. They followed him implicitly except on those occasions when bloodlust for penguins or seals made them oblivious. His former zest for sledging had left him and he would no longer wriggle his head into the harness, but on the other hand he would never run away from the harnessing as some dogs did.

We had many minor adventures with this team, through all of which my admiration of Stareek's character grew till I began to regard him as almost human, and longed for the time when I could give him rest and peace in civilisation. Sentiment was not a feeling which could be prominent in any friendship for Stareek, there was too much admiration in it and too little caressing. Nevertheless when I returned from a short absence from the base to find that Stareek had died, only three weeks before the ship was due, it was a real blow. The wise little puppy of the Amur was to remain in that distant land not far from his first and wisest driver, Dr Wilson, and all we could take back was the memory of his great character and a desire to pay tribute to him by telling his story, for he too deserves a place in the roll of honour of the great dogs in sledging history.

To a man the greatest blessing is individual liberty; to a dog it is the last word in despair.

William Lyon Phelps

Dorothy Parker

1894-1967

MR. DURANT
Excerpt

His children rushed, clamoring, to meet him, as he unlocked the door. There was something exciting going on, for Junior and Charlotte were usually too careful-mannered to cause people discomfort by rushing and babbling. They were nice, sensible children, good at their lessons, and punctilious about brushing their teeth, speaking the truth, and avoiding playmates who used bad words. Junior would be the very picture of his father, when they got the bands off his teeth, and little Charlotte strongly resembled her mother. Friends often commented on what a nice arrangement it was.

Mr. Durant smiled good-naturedly through their racket, carefully hanging up his coat and hat. There was even pleasure for him in the arrangement of his apparel on the cool, shiny knob of the hatrack. Everything was pleasant, tonight. Even the children's noise couldn't irritate him.

Eventually he discovered the cause of the commotion. It was a little stray dog that had come to the back door. They were out in the kitchen helping Freda, and Charlotte thought she heard something scratching, and Freda said nonsense, but Charlotte went to the door, anyway, and there was this little dog, trying to get in out of the wet. Mother helped them give it a bath, and Freda fed it, and now it was in the living room. Oh, Father, couldn't they keep it, please, couldn't they, couldn't they, please. Father, couldn't they? It didn't have any collar on it—so you see it didn't belong to anybody. Mother said all right, if he said so, and Freda liked it fine.

Mr. Durant still smiled his gentle smile. "We'll see," he said.

The children looked disappointed, but not despondent. They would have liked more enthusiasm, but "we'll see," they knew by experience, meant a leaning in the right direction.

Mr. Durant proceeded to the living-room, to inspect the visitor. It was not a beauty. All too obviously, it was the living souvenir of a mother who had never been able to say no. It was a rather stocky little beast with shaggy white hair and occasional, rakishly placed patches of black. There was a suggestion of Sealyham terrier about it, but that was almost blotted out by hosts of reminiscences of other breeds. It looked, on the whole, like a composite photograph of Popular Dogs. But you could tell at a glance that it had a way with it. Scepters have been tossed aside for that.

It lay, now, by the fire, waving its tragically long tail wistfully, its eyes pleading with Mr. Durant to give it a fair trial. The children had told it to lie down there, and so it did not move. That was something it could do toward repaying them.

Mr. Durant warmed to it. He did not dislike dogs, and he somewhat fancied the picture of himself as a soft-hearted fellow who extended shelter to friendless animals. He bent, and held out a hand to it.

"Well, sir," he said, genially. "Come here, good fellow."

The dog ran to him, wriggling ecstatically. It covered his cold hand with joyous, though respectful kisses, then laid its warm, heavy head on his palm. "You are beyond a doubt the greatest man in America," it told him with its eyes.

Mr. Durant enjoyed appreciation and gratitude. He patted the dog graciously.

"Well, sir, how'd you like to board with us?" he said. "I guess you can plan to settle down." Charlotte squeezed Junior's arm wildly. Neither of them, though, thought it best to crowd their good fortune by making any immediate comment on it.

Mrs. Durant entered from the kitchen, flushed with her final attentions to the chowder. There was a worried line between her eyes. Part of the worry was due to the dinner, and part to the disturbing entrance of the little dog into the family life. Anything not previously included in her day's schedule threw Mrs. Durant into a state resembling that of one convalescing from shellshock. Her hands jerked nervously, beginning gestures that they never finished.

Relief smoothed her face when she saw her husband patting the dog. The children, always at ease with her, broke their silence and jumped about her, shrieking that Father said it might stay.

"There, now—didn't I tell you what a dear, good father you had?" she said in the tone parents employ when they have happened to guess right. "That's fine, Father. With the big yard and all, I think we'll make out all right. She really seems to be an awfully good little———."

Mr. Durant's hand stopped sharply in its patting motions, as if the dog's neck had become red-hot to his touch. He rose, and looked at his wife as at a stranger who had suddenly begun to behave wildly.

"She?" he said. He maintained the look and repeated the word. "She?"

Mrs. Durant's hands jerked.

"Well—" she began, as if about to plunge into a recital of extenuating circumstances. "Well—yes," she concluded.

The children and the dog looked nervously at

105

Mr. Durant, feeling something was gone wrong. Charlotte whimpered wordlessly.

"Quiet!" said her father, turning suddenly upon her. "I said it could stay, didn't I? Did you ever know Father to break a promise?"

Charlotte politely murmured, "No, Father," but conviction was not hers. She was a philosophical child, though, and she decided to leave the whole issue to God, occasionally jogging Him up a bit with prayer.

Mr. Durant frowned at his wife, and jerked his head backward. This indicated that he wished to have a few words with her, for adults only, in the privacy of the little room across the hall, known as "Father's den."

He had directed the decoration of his den, had seen that it had been made a truly masculine room. Red paper covered its walls, up to the wooden rack on which were displayed ornamental steins, of domestic manufacture. Empty pipe-racks—Mr. Durant smoked cigars—were nailed against the red paper at frequent intervals. On one wall was an indifferent reproduction of a drawing of a young woman with wings like a vampire bat, and on another, a water-colored photograph of "September Morn," the tints running a bit beyond the edges of the figure as if the artist's emotions had rendered his hand unsteady. Over the table was carefully flung a tanned and fringed hide with the profile of an unknown Indian maiden painted on it, and the rocking-chair held a leather pillow bearing the picture, done by pyrography, of a girl in a fencing costume which set off her distressingly dated figure.

Mr. Durant's books were lined up behind the glass of the bookcase. They were all tall, thick books, brightly bound, and they justified his pride in their showing. They were mostly accounts of favorites of the French court, with a few volumes on odd personal habits of various monarchs, and the adventures of former Russian monks. Mrs. Durant, who never had time to get around to reading, regarded them with awe, and thought of her husband as one of the country's leading bibliophiles. There were books, too, in the living-room, but those she had inherited or been given. She had arranged a few on the living-room table; they looked as if they had been placed there by the Gideons.

Mr. Durant thought of himself as an indefatigable collector and an insatiable reader. But he was always disappointed in his books, after he had sent for them. They were never so good as the advertisements had led him to believe.

Into his den Mr. Durant preceded his wife, and faced her, still frowning. His calm was not shattered, but it was punctured. Something annoying always had to go and come up. Wouldn't you know?

"Now you know perfectly well, Fan, we can't have that dog around," he told her. He used the low voice reserved for underwear and bathroom articles and kindred shady topics. There was all the kindness in his tones that one has for a backward child, but a Gibraltar-like firmness was behind it. "You must be crazy to even think we could for a minute. Why, I wouldn't give a she-dog house-room, not for any amount of money. It's disgusting, that's what it is."

"Well, but, Father—" began Mrs. Durant, her hands again going off into their convulsions.

"Disgusting," he repeated. "You have a female around, and you know what happens. All the males in the neighborhood will be running after her. First thing you know, she'd be having puppies—and the way they look after they've had them, and all! That would be nice for the children to see, wouldn't it? I should think you'd think of the children, Fan. No, sir, there'll be nothing like that around here, not while I know it. Disgusting!"

"But the children," she said. "They'll be just simply———"

"Now you just leave all that to me," he reassured her. "I told them the dog could stay, and I've never broken a promise yet, have I? Here's what I'll do— I'll wait till they're asleep, and then I'll just take this little dog and put it out. Then, in the morning, you can tell them it ran away during the night, see?"

She nodded. Her husband patted her shoulder, in its crapy-smelling black silk. His peace with the world was once more intact, restored by this simple solution of the little difficulty. Again his mind wrapped itself in the knowledge that everything was all fixed, all ready for a nice, fresh start. His arm was still about his wife's shoulder as they went on in to dinner.

We are alone, absolutely alone on this chance planet, and, amid all the forms of life that surround us, not one, excepting the dog, has made an alliance with us.
Maurice Maeterlinck

When a dog wants to hang out the 'Do Not Disturb' sign, as all of us do now and then, he is regarded as a traitor to his species.
Romona C. Albert

There is no doubt that every healthy, normal boy (if there is such a thing in these days of Child Study) should own a dog at some time in his life, preferably between the ages of 45 and 50. *Robert Benchley*

E. B. White

1889-

THE CARE AND TRAINING OF A DOG

There is a book out called *Dog Training Made Easy* and it was sent to me the other day by the publisher, who rightly guessed that it would catch my eye. I like to read books on dog training. Being the owner of dachshunds, to me a book on dog discipline becomes a volume of inspired humor. Every sentence is a riot. Some day, if I ever get a chance, I shall write a book, or warning, on the character and temperament of the dachshund and why he can't be trained and shouldn't be. I would rather train a striped zebra to balance an Indian club than induce a dachshund to heed my slightest command. For a number of years past I have been agreeably encumbered by a very large and dissolute dachshund named Fred. Of all the dogs whom I have served I've never known one who understood so much of what I say or held it in such deep contempt. When I address Fred I never have to raise either my voice or my hopes. He even disobeys me when I instruct him in something that he wants to do. And when I answer his peremptory scratch at the door and hold the door open for him to walk through, he stops in the middle and lights a cigarette, just to hold me up.

"Shopping for a puppy presents a number of problems," writes Mr. Wm. Cary Duncan, author of *Dog Training Made Easy.* Well, shopping for a puppy has never presented many problems for me, as most of the puppies and dogs that have entered my life (and there have been scores of them) were not the result of a shopping trip but of an act of God. The first puppy I owned, when I was about nine years old, was not shopped for—it was born to the collie bitch of the postman of my older sister, who sent it to me by express from Washington, D.C., in a little crate containing, in addition to the puppy, a bar of Peters' chocolate and a ripe frankfurter. And the puppy I own now was not shopped for but was won in a raffle. Between these two extremes there have been many puppies, mostly unshopped for. It is not so much that I acquire dogs as it is that dogs acquire me. Maybe they even shop for me, I don't know. If they do I assume they have many problems, because they certainly always arrive with plenty, which they then turn over to me.

The possession of a dog to-day is a different thing from the possession of a dog at the turn of the century, when one's dog was fed on mashed potato and brown gravy and lived in a doghouse with an arched portal. To-day a dog is fed on scraped beef and Vitamin B1 and lives in bed with you.

An awful lot of nonsense has been written about dogs by persons who don't know them very well and the attempt to elevate the purebred to a position of national elegance has been, in the main, a success. Dogs used to mate with other dogs rather casually in my day, and the results were discouraging to the American Kennel Club but entirely satisfactory to small boys who liked puppies. In my suburban town, "respectable" people didn't keep she-dogs. One's washer-woman might keep a bitch, or one's lawn cutter, but not one's next-door neighbor.

The prejudice against females made a deep impression on me, and I grew up thinking that there was something indecent and unclean about she-things in general. The word bitch of course was never used in polite families. One day a little mutt followed me home from school, and after much talk I persuaded my parents to let me keep it—at least until the owner turned up or advertised for it. It dwelt among us only one night. Next morning my father took me aside and in a low voice asid: "My son, I don't know whether you realize it, but that dog is a female. It'll have to go."

"But why does it have to?" I asked.

"They're a nuisance," he replied, embarrassed "We'd have all the other dogs in the neighborhood around here all the time."

That sounded like an idyllic arrangement to me, but I could tell from my father's voice that the stray dog was doomed. We turned her out and she went off toward the more liberal section of town. This sort of incident must have been happening to thousands of American youngsters in those days, and we grew up to find that it had been permanently added to the record by Dorothy Parker in her short story "Mr. Durant."

On our block, in the days of my innocence, there were in addition to my collie, a pug dog, a dachshund named Bruno, a fox terrier named Sunny who spent many years studying one croquet ball, a red setter, and a St. Bernard who carried his mistress's handbag, shuffling along in a stately fashion with the drool running out both sides of his jaws. I was scared of this St. Bernard because of his size, and never passed his house without dread. The dachshund was old, surly, and disagreeable, and was endlessly burying bones in the flower border of the DeVries's yard. I should very much doubt if any of those animals ever had its temperature taken rectally, ever was fed raw meat or tomato juice, ever was given distemper inoculations, or ever saw the whites of a veterinary's eyes. They were brought up on chicken bones and gravy and left-over cereal, and were all fine dogs. Most never saw the inside of the owner's house—they knew their place.

The "problem" of caring for a dog has been unnecessarily complicated. Take the matter of housebreaking. In the suburbia of those lovely post-Victorian days of which I write the question of housebreaking a puppy was met with the simple bold courage characteristic of our forefathers. You simply kept the house away from the puppy. This was not only the simplest way, it was the only practical way, just as it is to-day. Our parents were in possession of a vital secret—a secret which has been all but lost to the world: the knowledge that a puppy will live and thrive without ever crossing the threshold of a dwelling house, at least till he's big enough so he doesn't wet the rug.

Although our fathers and mothers very sensibly never permitted a puppy to come into the house, they made up for this indignity by always calling the puppy "Sir." In those days a dog didn't expect anything very elaborate in the way of food or medical care, but he did expect to be addressed civilly.

Mr. Duncan discusses housebreaking at some length and assumes, as do all writers of dog books, that the owner of a puppy has little else to do except own the puppy. It is Mr. Duncan's theory that puppies have a sense of modesty and don't like to be stared at when they are doing something. When you are walking the dog, he says, you must "appear utterly uninterested" as you approach some favorite spot. This, as any city dweller knows, is a big order. Nothing is more comical than the look on the face of a person at the upper end of a dog leash, pretending not to know what is going on at the lower.

A really companionable and indispensable dog is an accident of nature. You can't get it by breeding for it, and you can't buy it with money. It just happens along. Out of the vast sea of assorted dogs that I have had dealings with, by far the noblest, the best, and the most important was the first, the one my sister sent me in a crate. He was an old-style collie, beautifully marked, with a blunt nose, and great natural gentleness and intelligence. When I got him he was what I badly needed. I think probably all these other dogs of mine have been just a groping toward that old dream. I've never dared get another collie for fear the comparison would be too uncomfortable. I can still see my first dog in all the moods and situations that memory has filed him away in, but I think of him oftenest as he used to be right after breakfast on the back porch, listlessly eating up a dish of petrified oatmeal rather than hurt my feelings. For six years he met me at the same place after school and convoyed me home—a service he thought up himself. A boy doesn't forget that sort of association. It is a monstrous trick of fate that now, settled in the country and with sheep to take care of, I am obliged to do my shepherding with the grotesque and sometimes underhanded assistance of two dachshunds and a wire-haired fox terrier.

James Herriot

1916-

ALL CREATURES
GREAT AND SMALL
Excerpt

I looked again at the slip of paper where I had written my visits. "Dean, 3, Thompson's Yard. Old dog ill."

There were a lot of these "yards" in Darrowby. They were, in fact, tiny streets, like pictures from a Dickens novel. Some of them opened off the market place and many more were scattered behind the main thoroughfares in the old part of the town. From the outside you could see only an archway and it was always a surprise to me to go down a narrow passage and come suddenly upon the uneven rows of little houses with no two alike, looking into each other's windows across eight feet of cobbles.

In front of some of the houses a strip of garden had been dug out and marigolds and nasturtiums straggled over the rough stones; but at the far end the houses were in a tumble-down condition and some were abandoned with their windows boarded up.

Number three was down at this end and looked as though it wouldn't be able to hold out much longer.

The flakes of paint quivered on the rotten wood of the door as I knocked; above, the outer wall bulged dangerously on either side of a long crack in the masonry.

A small, white-haired man answered. His face, pinched and lined, was enlivened by a pair of cheerful eyes; he wore a much-darned woollen cardigan, patched trousers and slippers.

"I've come to see your dog," I said, and the old man smiled.

"Oh, I'm glad you've come, sir," he said. "I'm getting a bit worried about the old chap. Come inside, please."

He led me into the tiny living-room. "I'm alone now, sir. Lost my missus over a year ago. She used to think the world of the old dog."

The grim evidence of poverty was everywhere. In the worn out lino, the fireless hearth, the dank, musty smell of the place. The wallpaper hung away from the damp patches and on the table the old man's solitary dinner was laid; a fragment of bacon, a few fried potatoes and a cup of tea. This was life on the old age pension.

In the corner, on a blanket, lay my patient, a crossbred labrador. He must have been a big powerful dog in his time, but the signs of age showed in the white hairs around his muzzle and the pale opacity in the depth of his eyes. He lay quietly and looked at me without hostility.

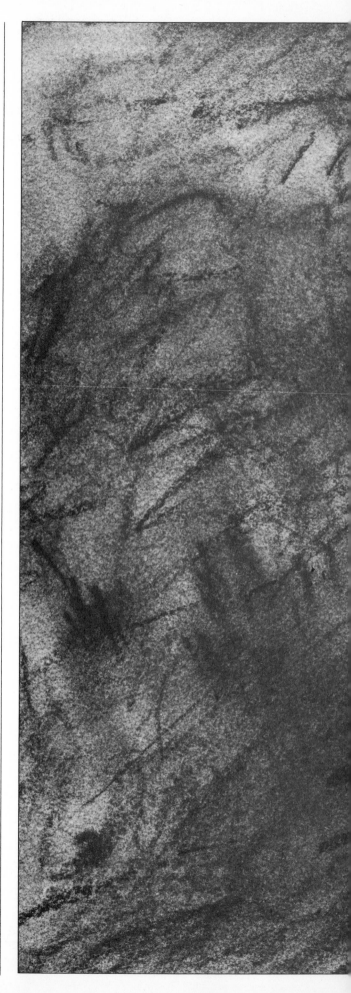

"Getting on a bit, isn't he, Mr. Dean?"

"Aye he is that. Nearly fourteen, but he's been like a pup galloping about until these last few weeks. Wonderful dog for his age, is old Bob and he's never offered to bite anybody in his life. Children can do anything with him. He's my only friend now—I hope you'll soon be able to put him right."

"Is he off his food, Mr. Dean?"

"Yes, clean off, and that's a strange thing because, by gum, he could eat. He always sat by me and put his head on my knee at meal times, but he hasn't been doing it lately."

I looked at the dog with growing uneasiness. The abdomen was grossly distended and I could read the telltale symptoms of pain; the catch in the respirations, the retracted commissures of the lips, the anxious, preoccupied expression in the eyes.

When his master spoke, the tail thumped twice on the blankets and a momentary interest showed in the white old eyes; but it quickly disappeared and the blank, inward look returned.

I passed my hand carefully over the dog's abdomen. Ascites was pronounced and the dropsical fluid had gathered till the pressure was intense. "Come on, old cap," I said "let's see if we can roll you over." The dog made no resistance as I eased him slowly on to his other side, but, just as the movement was completed, he whimpered and looked round. The cause of the trouble was now only too easy to find.

I palpated gently. Through the thin muscle of the flank I could feel a hard, corrugated mass; certainly a splenic or hepatic carcinoma, enormous and completely inoperable. I stroked the old dog's head as I tried to collect my thoughts. This wasn't going to be easy.

"Is he going to be ill for long?" the old man asked, and again came the thump, thump of the tail at the sound of the loved voice. "It's miserable when Bob isn't following me round the house when I'm doing my little jobs."

"I'm sorry, Mr. Dean, but I'm afraid this is something very serious. You see this large swelling. It is caused by an internal growth."

"You mean...cancer?" the little man said faintly.

"I'm afraid so, and it has progressed too far for anything to be done. I wish there was something I could do to help him, but there isn't.

The old man looked bewildered and his lips trembled. "Then he's going to die?"

I swallowed hard, "We really can't just leave him to die, can we? He's in some distress now, but it will soon be an awful lot worse. Don't you think it would be kindest to put him to sleep? After all, he's had a good, long innings." I always aimed at a brisk, matter-of-fact approach, but the old cliches had an empty

ring.

The old man was silent, then he said, "Just a minute," and slowly and painfully knelt down by the side of the dog. He did not speak, but ran his hand again and again over the grey old muzzle and the ears, while the tail thump, thump, thumped on the floor.

He knelt there a long time while I stood in the cheerless room, my eyes taking in the faded pictures on the walls, the frayed, grimy curtains, the broken-springed armchair.

At length the old man struggled to his feet and gulped once or twice. Without looking at me, he said huskily, "All right, will you do it now?"

I filled the syringe and said the things I always said. "You needn't worry, this is absolutely painless. Just an overdose of an anaesthetic. It is really an easy way out for the old fellow."

The dog did not move as the needle was inserted, and, as the barbiturate began to flow into the vein, the anxious expression left his face and the muscles began to relax. By the time the injection was finished, the breathing had stopped.

"Is that it?" the old man whispered.

"Yes, that's it," I said. "He is out of his pain now."

The old man stood motionless except for the clasping and unclasping of his hands. When he turned to face me his eyes were bright. "That's right, we couldn't let him suffer and I'm grateful for what you've done. And now, what do I owe you for your services, sir?"

"Oh, that's all right, Mr. Dean," I said quickly. "It's nothing—nothing at all. I was passing right by here —it was no trouble."

The old man was astonished. "But you can't do that for nothing."

"Now please say no more about it, Mr. Dean. As I told you, I was passing right by your door." I said goodbye and went out of the house, through the passage and into the street. In the bustle of people and the bright sunshine, I could still see only the stark, little room, the old man and his dead dog.

As I walked towards my car, I heard a shout behind me. The old man was shuffling excitedly towards me in his slippers. His cheeks were streaked and wet, but he was smiling. In his hand he held a small, brown object.

"You've been very kind, sir. I've got something for you." He held out the object and I looked at it. It was tattered but just recognisable as a precious relic of a bygone celebration.

"Go on, it's for you," said the old man. "Have a cigar."

Every dog is entitled to one bite.   *Anonymous*

James Thurber

1894-1961

THE STORY OF BARGE

There once lived in Columbus, Ohio, on Franklin Avenue, a dog named Barge. He was an average kind of dog, medium in size and weight, ordinary in markings. His master and mistress and their two children made up a respectable middle-class family. Some of the young men of the neighbourhood, however, pool-shooting, motor-cycle-riding bravos, lured Barge into a saloon one day and set before him a saucer of beer. He lapped it up and liked it. From there it was but an easy step to whisky.

Barge was terribly funny, the boys thought, when he got stiff. He would bump into things, hiccup, grin foolishly, and even raise his muzzle on high in what passed for 'Sweet Adeline.' Barge's coat became shabby, his gait uncertain, and his eyes misty. He took to staying out in the town all night, raising hell. His duties as watchdog in the home of his owners were completely neglected. One night, when Barge was off on one of his protracted bats, burglars broke in and made off with his mistress's best silver and cut glass.

Barge, staggering home around noon of the next day, sniffed disaster when he was still a block away. His owners were waiting for him grimly on the front porch. They had not straightened up after the bur-

glars. The sideboard drawers were pulled out, the floor littered with napkins and napkin rings. Barge's ears, chops, and tail fell as he was led sternly into the house to behold the result of his wicked way of life. He took one long, sad look around, and the cloudiness cleared from his head. He realised that he was not only a ne'er-do-well but a wrongo. One must guard the house at night, warn the family of fire, pull drowning infants out of the lake. These were the sacred trusts, the inviolable laws. Man had dragged Barge very far down, but there was still a spark of doghood left in him. He ran quickly upstairs, jumped out of an open window, and killed himself. This is a true and solemn legend of Franklin Avenue.

THE SCOTTY WHO KNEW TOO MUCH

Several summers ago there was a Scotty who went to the country for a visit. He decided that all the farm dogs were cowards, because they were afraid of a certain animal that had a white stripe down its back. "You are a pussy-cat and I can lick you," the Scotty said to the farm dog who lived in the house where the Scotty was visiting. "I can lick the little animal with the white stripe, too. Show him to me." "Don't you want to ask any questions about him?" said the farm dog. "Naw," said the Scotty "*You* ask the questions."

So the farm dog took the Scotty into the woods and showed him the white-striped animal and the Scotty closed in on him, growling and slashing. It was all over in a moment and the Scotty lay on his back. When he came to, the farm dog said, "What happened?" "He threw vitriol," said the Scotty, "but he never laid a glove on me."

A few days later the farm dog told the Scotty there was another animal all the farm dogs were afraid of. "Lead me to him," said the Scotty. "I can lick anything that doesn't wear horseshoes." "Don't you want to ask any questions about him?" said the farm dog. "Naw," said the Scotty. "Just show me where he hangs out." So the farm dog led him to a place in the woods and pointed out the little animal when he came along. "A clown," said the Scotty, "a pushover," and he closed in, leading with his left and exhibiting some mighty fancy footwork. In less than a second the Scotty was flat on his back, and when he woke up the farm dog was pulling quills out of him. "What happened?" said the farm dog. "He pulled a knife on me," said the Scotty, "but at least I have learned how you fight out here in the country, and now I am going to beat *you* up." So he closed in on the farm dog, holding his nose with one front paw to ward off the vitriol and covering his eyes with the other front paw to keep out the knives. The Scotty couldn't see his opponent and he couldn't smell his opponent and he was so badly beaten that he had to be taken back to the city and put in a nursing home.

Moral: It is better to ask some of the questions than to know all the answers.

THE DOG THAT BIT PEOPLE

Probably no one man should have as many dogs in his life as I have had, but there was more pleasure than distress in them for me except in the case of an Airedale named Muggs. He gave me more trouble than all the other fifty-four or -five put together, although my moment of keenest embarrassment was the time a Scotch terrier named Jeannie, who had just had four puppies in the shoe closet of a fourth-floor apartment in New York, had the fifth and last at the corner of—but we shall get around to that later on. Then, too, there was the prize-winning French poodle, a great big black poodle—none of your little, untroublesome white miniatures—who got sick riding in the rumble seat of a car with me on her way to the Greenwich Dog Show. She had a red rubber bib tucked around her throat and, since a rain-storm came up when we were halfway through the Bronx, I had to hold over her a small green umbrella, really more of a parasol. The rain beat down fearfully, and suddenly the driver of the car drove into a big garage, filled with mechanics. It happened so quickly that I forgot to put the umbrella down, and I shall always remember the look of incredulity that came over the face of the garageman who came over to see what we wanted. "Get a load of this, Mac," he called to someone behind him.

But the Airedale, as I have said, was the worst of all my dogs. He really wasn't my dog, as a matter of fact; I came home from a vacation one summer to find that my brother Robert had bought him while I was away. A big, burly, choleric dog, he always acted as if he thought I wasn't one of the family. There was a slight advantage in being one of the family, for he didn't bite the family as often as he bit strangers. Still, in the years that we had him he bit everybody but Mother, and he made a pass at her once but missed. That was during the month when we suddenly had mice, and Muggs refused to do anything about them. Nobody ever had mice exactly like the mice we had that month. They acted like pet mice, almost like mice somebody had trained. They were so friendly that one night when Mother entertained at dinner the Friraliras, a club she and my father had belonged to for twenty years, she put down a lot of little dishes with food in them on the pantry floor so that the mice would be satisfied with that and wouldn't come into the dining room. Muggs stayed out in the pantry with the mice, lying on the floor, growling to himself—not at the mice, but about all the people in the next room that he would have liked to get at. Mother slipped out into the pantry once to see how everything was going. Everything was going fine. It made her so mad to see Muggs lying there, oblivious of the mice—they came running up to her—that she slapped him and he slashed at her, but didn't make it. He was sorry immediately, Mother said. He was always sorry, she said, after he bit someone, but we could not understand how she figured this out. He didn't act sorry.

Mother used to send a box of candy every Christmas to the people the Airedale bit. The list finally contained forty or more names. Nobody could understand why we didn't get rid of the dog. I didn't understand it very well myself, but we didn't get rid of him. I think that one or two people tried to poison Muggs—he acted poisoned once in a while—and old Major Moberly fired at him once with his service revolver near the Seneca Hotel in Easy Broad Street—but Muggs lived to be almost eleven years old, and even when he could hardly get around, he bit a congressman who had called to see my father on business. My mother had never liked the congressman—she said the signs of his horoscope showed he couldn't be trusted (he was Saturn with the moon in Virgo)—but she sent him a box of candy that Christmas. He sent it right back, probably because he suspected it was trick candy. Mother persuaded herself it was all for the best that the dog had bitten him, even though father lost an important business association because of it. "I wouldn't be associated with such a man," Mother said. "Muggs could read him like a book."

We used to take turns feeding Muggs to be on his good side, but that didn't always work. He was never in a very good humor, even after a meal. Nobody knew exactly what was the matter with him, but whatever it was it made him irascible, especially in the mornings. Robert never felt very well in the morning, either, especially before breakfast, and once when he came downstairs and found that Muggs had moodily chewed up the morning paper he hit him in the face with a grapefruit and then jumped on the dining-room table, scattering dishes and silverware and spilling the coffee. Muggs' first leap carried him all the way across the table and into a brass fire screen in front of the gas grate, but he was back on his feet in a moment, and in the end he got Robert and gave him a pretty vicious bite in the leg. Then he was all over it; he never bit anyone more than once at a time. Mother always mentioned that as an argument in his favor; she said he had a quick temper but that he didn't hold a grudge. She was forever defending him. I think she liked him because he wasn't well. "He's not strong," she would say, pityingly, but that was inaccurate; he may not have been well but he was terribly strong.

One time my mother went to the Chittenden Hotel to call on a woman mental healer who was lecturing in Columbus on the subject of "Harmonious Vibrations." She wanted to find out if it was possible to get harmonious vibrations into a dog. "He's a large tan-colored Airedale," Mother explained. The woman said she had never treated a dog, but she advised my mother to hold the thought that he did not bite and would not bite. Mother was holding the thought the very next morning when Muggs got the iceman, but she blamed that slip-up on the iceman. "If you didn't think he would bite you, he wouldn't," Mother told him. He stomped out of the house in a terrible jangle of vibrations.

One morning when Muggs bit me slightly, more or less in passing, I reached down and grabbed his short stumpy tail and hoisted him into the air. It was a foolhardy thing to do and the last time I saw my mother, about six months ago, she said she didn't know what possessed me. I don't either, except that I was pretty mad. As long as I held the dog off the floor by his tail he couldn't get at me, but he twisted and jerked so, snarling all the time, that I realized I couldn't hold him that way very long. I carried him to the kitchen and flung him onto the floor and shut the door on him just as he crashed against it. But I forgot about the back stairs. Muggs went up the back stairs and down the front stairs and had me

cornered in the living room. I managed to get up onto the mantelpiece above the fireplace, but it gave way and came down with a tremendous crash, throwing a large marble clock, several vases, and myself heavily to the floor. Muggs was so alarmed by the racket that when I picked myself up he had disappeared. We couldn't find him anywhere, although we whistled and shouted, until old Mrs. Detweiler called after dinner that night. Muggs had bitten her once, in the leg, and she came into the living room only after we assured her that Muggs had run away. She had just seated herself when, with a great growling and scratching of claws, Muggs emerged from under a davenport where he had been quietly hiding all the time, and bit her again. Mother examined the bite and put arnica on it and told Mrs. Detweiler that it was only a bruise. "He just bumped you," she said. But Mrs. Detweiler left the house in a nasty state of mind.

Lots of people reported our Airedale to the police, but my father held a municipal office at the time and was on friendly terms with the police. Even so, the cops had been out a couple of times—once when Muggs bit Mrs. Rufus Sturtevant and again when he bit Lieutenant-Governor Malloy—but Mother told them that it hadn't been Muggs' fault but the fault of the people who were bitten. "When he starts for them, they scream," she explained, "and that excites him." The cops suggested that it might be a good idea to tie the dog up, but Mother said that it mortified him to be tied up and that he wouldn't eat when he was tied up.

Muggs at his meals was an unusual sight. Because of the fact that if you reached toward the floor he would bite you, we usually put his food plate on top of an old kitchen table with a bench alongside the table. Muggs would stand on the bench and eat. I remember that my mother's Uncle Horatio, who boasted that he was the third man up Missionary Ridge, was splutteringly indignant when he found out that we fed the dog on a table because we were afraid to put his plate on the floor. He said he wasn't afraid of any dog that ever lived and that he would put the dog's plate on the floor it we would give it to him. Robert said that if Uncle Horatio had fed Muggs on the ground just before the battle he would have been the first man up Missionary Ridge. Uncle Horatio was furious. "Bring him in! Bring him in now!" he shouted. "I'll feed the——on the floor!" Robert was all for giving him a chance, but my father wouldn't hear of it. He said that Muggs had already been fed. "I'll feed him again!" bawled Uncle Horatio. We had quite a time quieting him.

In his last year Muggs used to spend practically all of his time outdoors. He didn't like to stay in the house for some reason or other—perhaps it held too many unpleasant memories for him. Anyway, it was hard to get him to come in, and as a result the garbage man, the iceman, and the laundryman wouldn't come near the house. We had to haul the garbage down to the corner, take the laundry out and bring it back, and meet the iceman a block from home. After this had gone on for some time, we hit on an ingenious arrangement for getting the dog in the house so that we could lock him up while the gas meter was read, and so on. Muggs was afraid of only one thing, an electrical storm. Thunder and lightning frightened him out of his senses (I think he thought a storm had broken the day the mantelpiece fell). He would rush into the house and hide under a bed or in a clothes closet. So we fixed up a thunder machine out of a long narrow piece of sheet iron with a wooden handle on one end. Mother would shake this vigorously when she wanted to get Muggs into the house. It made an excellent imitation of thunder, but I suppose it was the most roundabout system for running a household that was ever devised. It took a lot out of Mother.

A few months before Muggs died, he got to "seeing things." He would rise slowly from the floor, growling low, and stalk stiff-legged and menacing toward nothing at all. Sometimes the Thing would be just a little to the right or left of a visitor. Once a Fuller Brush salesman got hysterics. Muggs came wandering into the room like Hamlet following his father's ghost. His eyes were fixed on a spot just to the left of the Fuller Brush man, who stood it until Muggs was about three slow, creeping paces from him. Then he shouted. Muggs wavered on past him into the hallway, grumbling to himself, but the Fuller Brush man went on shouting. I think Mother had to throw a pan of cold water on him before he stopped. That was the way she used to stop us boys when we got into fights.

Muggs died quite suddenly one night. Mother wanted to bury him in the family plot under a marble stone with some such inscription as "Flights of angels sing thee to thy rest" but we persuaded her it was against the law. In the end we just put up a smooth board above his grave along a lonely road. On the board I wrote with an indelible pencil "*Cave Canem*." Mother was quite pleased with the simple, classic dignity of the old Latin epitaph.

Richard M. Nixon

1913-

THE CHECKERS
SPEECH 1952

|O|ne other thing I probably should tell you, because if I don't they'll probably be saying this about me too. We did get something, a gift, after the election. A man down in Texas heard Pat on the radio mention the fact that our two youngsters would like to have a dog. And, believe it or not, the day before we left on this campaign trip we got a message from Union Station in Baltimore saying they had a package for us. We went down to get it. You know what it was? It was a little cocker spaniel dog in a crate that he sent all the way from Texas. Black and white spotted. And our little girl Tricia, the six-year old, named it Checkers. And you know, the kids love the dog, and I just want to say this right now, that regardless of what they say about it, we're gonna keep it.

Mikhail Bulgakov

1891-1940

HEART OF A DOG
Excerpts

Whoo-oo-oo-hooh-hoo-oo! Oh, look at me, I am perishing in this gateway. The blizzard roars a prayer for the dying, and I howl with it. I am finished, finished. That bastard in the dirty cap—the cook of the Normal Diet Cafeteria for employees of the People's Central Economic Soviet—threw boiling water at me and scalded my left side. The scum, and he calls himself a proletarian! Lord, o lord, how it hurts! hurts! my side is cooked to the bone. And now I howl and howl, but what's the good of howling?

What harm did I do him? Would the People's Economic Soviet get any poorer if I rooted in the garbage heap? The greedy brute! Take a look at that mug of his sometimes—it's wider than it's long. A crook with a brass jowl. Ah, people, people! It was at noontime that Dirty Cap gave me a taste of boiling water, and now it's getting dark, it must be about four in the afternoon, judging from the smell of onions from the Prechistenka fire-house...

...Time and again. I've tasted everything, but I've made peace with my fate, and if I'm whining now, it's only because of the pain and the cold—because my spirit hasn't yet gone out of my body....A dog is hard to kill, his spirit clings to life...

...The door of the brightly lit store across the street swung open and a citizen came out of it. Yes, precisely, a citizen, not a comrade. Or even, to be more exact, a gentleman. The closer he came, the clearer it was...

...The dog crawled on his belly like a snake, weeping bitter tears. *Observe the cook's work. But you'll never give me anything. Oh, I know the rich very well! But actually, what do you need it for? What do you want with putrid horsemeat? You'll never get such poison as they sell you at the Moscow Agricultural Industries stores anywhere else. And you have had your lunch today, you, a personage of world importance, thanks to male sex glands. Oo-oo-oo-oo...What's happening in this world? But it seems too early to die, and despair is truly a sin. I must lick his hands, there's nothing else left...*

...The mysterious gentleman bent over the dog, the gold rims of his glasses flashed, and he took a long, white package from his right pocket. Without removing his brown gloves, he unwrapped the paper, which was immediately snatched up by the blizzard, and broke off a piece of what is known as "special Cracow sausage." And he held it out to the dog. *Oh, generous soul! Oo-oo-oo!*

"Whuit-whuit," the gentleman whistled and added in the sternest tone: "Take it! Sharik, Sharik!"

Sharik again. They'd christened me. But call me what you will. For such an exceptional deed!

The dog instantly pulled off the skin, sank his teeth with a sob into the Cracow sausage, and gobbled it up in a wink. And almost choked to tears on the sausage and the snow, because in his greed he had almost swallowed the cord. *I'll lick your hand now, again, again. I kiss your trousers, my benefactor!*

"Enough for now.." The gentleman spoke curtly, as though issuing commands. He bent down to Sharik, peered into his eyes, and suddenly passed his gloved hand intimately and caressingly over Sharik's belly.

"Ah," he said significantly. "No collar. That's fine, you're just what I need. Come on, follow me." He snapped his fingers, "Whuit, whuit!"

Follow you? Why, to the end of the world. You may kick me with your fine suede shoes, I wouldn't say a word.

The street lights gleamed all along the Prechistenka. His side ached intolerably, but Sharik forgot the pain from time to time, possessed by a single thought: he must not lose the wonderful vision in the overcoat in the crowd, he must do something to express his love and devotion. And he expressed it seven times along the stretch of Prechistenka up to Obukhov Lane. At Dead Man's Alley he kissed the man's overshoe. He cleared the way for him. Once he frightened a lady so badly with his wild howl that she plopped down on a fire pump. Twice he whimpered, to keep alive the man's sympathy for him.

A mangy stray tom, pretending to be Siberian, dived out from behind a drainpipe; he had caught a whiff of the sausage despite the storm. Sharik went blind with rage at the thought that the rich eccentric who picked up wounded mutts in gateways might take it into his head to bring along that thief as well, and then he'd be obliged to share the product of the Moscow Agricultural Industries with him. He snapped his teeth at the tom so furiously that the tom shot up the drainpip to the second story, hissing like a torn hose. *Gr-r-r-r...Wow! Feed every ragged tramp hanging around the Prechistenka!*

The gentleman appreciated his devotion: as they reach the firehouse, he stopped by the window from which the pleasant rumbling of a French horn could be heard and rewarded him with a second piece, a bit smaller, just a couple of ounces.

Ah, the silly man. He's trying to tempt me on. Don't worry, I won't run off. I'll follow you anywhere you say.

118

"Whuit-whuit-whuit! Here!"

Obukhove Lane? Certainly. I know the lane very well.

The unknown gentleman who had brought the dog to the doors of his luxurious apartment on the second floor rang, and the dog immediately raised his eyes to the large black card with gold letters next to the wide door with panes of wavy pink glass. He put together the first three letters right away: Pe-ar-o, "Pro." After that came a queer little hooked stick, nasty looking, unfamiliar. No telling what it meant. Could it be "proletarian"? Sharik wondered with astonishment …No, impossible. He raised his nose, sniffed the coat again, and said to himself with certainty: Oh, no, there's nothing proletarian in this smell. Some fancy, learned word, who knows what it means.

A sudden, joyous light flared up behind the pink glass, setting off the black card still more clearly. The door swung open silently, and a pretty young woman in a white apron and a lace cap appeared before the dog and his master. The former felt a gust of divine warmth, and the fragrance of lilies of the valley came at him from the woman's skirt.

That's something, that's really something, thought the dog.

"Come in, please, Mr. Sharik," the gentleman invited him ironically, and Sharik stepped in reverently, wagging his tail.

A multitude of objects crowded the rich foyer. He was most impressed with the mirror from the floor to

ceiling, which immediately reflected a second bedraggled, lacerated Sharik, the terrifying stag's horns up above, the numerous overcoats and boots, and the opalescent tulip with an electric light under the ceiling.

"Where did you dig him up, Philip Philippovich?" the woman asked, smiling and helping the gentleman to remove his heavy overcoat lined with silver fox, shimmering with bluish glints. "Heavens! What a mangy cur!"

"Nonsense. Where is he mangy?" the gentleman rapped out sternly.

Having removed the coat, he was now seen wearing a black suit of English cloth, with a gold chain gleaming discreetly and pleasantly across his stomach.

"Wait, stop wriggling, whuit…stop wriggling, you silly. Hm!…This isn't mange…wait a minute, you devil…Hm! A-ah. It's a burn. What scoundrel did it to you? Eh? Be still a moment, will you!…"

A cook, a bastard of a cook! The dog said with his piteous eyes and whimpered a little.

"Zina," commanded the gentleman, "take him to the examination room at once, and get me a smock."

The woman whistled, snapped her fingers, and the dog, after a moment's hesitation, followed her. They came into a narrow, dimly lit hallway, passed one laquered door, walked to the end, turned left, and found themselves in a dark little room which the dog immediately disliked for its ominous smell. The darkness clicked and turned into blinding daylight, and he was dazzled by the glitter, shine, and whiteness all around.

Oh, no, the dog howled mentally. Excuse me, but I won't, won't let you! Now I understand it, to hell with them and their sausage. They've tricked me into a dog hospital. Now they'll make me lap castor oil, and cut up my whole side with knives, and I cannot bear to have it touched as it is.

"Hey, stop, where are you going?" cried the woman called Zina.

The dog spun around, coiled himself like a spring, and suddenly threw himself at the door with his sound side so that the crash was heard all through the apartment. Then he sprang back and whirled on the spot like a top, turning over a white pail and sending the tufts of cotton it contained flying in all directions. As he spun, the walls lined with cases full of glittering instruments danced around him; the white apron and the screaming, distorted female face bobbed up and down.

"Where do you think you're going, you shaggy devil?" Zina cried desperately. "Damned cur!"

Where is their back staircase? wondered the dog.

He dashed himself at random at a glass door, hoping it was a second exit. A shower of splinters scattered, ringing and clattering, then a potbellied jar flew out, and the reddish muck in it instantly spread over the floor, raising a stench. The real door flew open.

"Wait, you brute," shouted the gentleman, jumping around, with one arm in the sleeve of the smock, trying to catch the dog by the leg. "Zina, grab him by the scruff, the bastard!"

"My…oh, my, what a dog!"

The door opened still wider and another male individual in a smock burst in. Crushing the broken glass, he rushed, not to the dog, but to an instrument case, opened it, and the whole room filled with a sweetish, nauseating smell. Then the individual threw himself upon the dog, pressing him down with his belly; in the course of the struggle the dog managed to snap enthusiastically at his leg just above the shoe. The individual gasped, but did not lose control. The nauseous liquid stopped the dog's breath and his head began to reel. Then his legs dropped off, and he slid off somewhere sideways. Thank you, it's all over, he thought dreamily, dropping right on the sharp splinters. Goodbye Moscow! Never again will I see Chichkin's and proletarians and Cracow sausage. I'm off to paradise for my long patience in this dog's life. Brothers, murderers, why are you doing it to me?

And he rolled over on his side and gave up the ghost.

When he revived, his head was turning vaguely and he had a queasy feeling at the pit of his stomach. As for his side, it did not exist, his side was blissfully silent. The dog opened his languorous right eye and saw out of the corner of it that he was tightly bandaged across the sides and stomach. So they've had their will of me, the sons of bitches, after all, he thought mistily. It was a neat job, though, in all justice.

Mad dogs and Englishmen go out in the mid-day sun.
Noel Coward

Fox-terriers are born with about four times as much original sin in them as other dogs. *Jerome K. Jerome*

Things that upset a terrier may pass virtually unnoticed by a Great Dane. *Smiley Blanton*

If dogs could talk, perhaps we could find it as hard to get along with them as we do with people.
Karel Capek

Raymond A. Sokolov

1941-

MAN BITES DOG FOODS AND FINDS SOME ARE TO HIS LIKING

Every night in this country, 32,600,000 dogs eat dinner. So do about 20,000,000 cats. And more and more of them every year are eating commercial pet food. Americans will spend $1.5-billion for 6 billion pounds of pellets and kibble and dog biscuits—much more than the $390-million spent on baby food—without having the slightest idea of what is in the miserable-looking slop or how it tastes.

Not to worry. Veterinary researchers insist that more is known about dog and cat nutritional requirements than about human needs. The perfect pet diet, they say, is already in supermarkets. And a recent canine-human dog food tasting session indicated that, however awful it looks, most commercial dog food is no worse than bad hamburger.

The only trouble with most dogs' diets is what people feel compelled to put in them. Animal scientists seem to agree that all would be well if normally healthy dogs were simply given unlimited access to nothing but commercial dry food and water and nothing else. Table scraps and "all-meat" canned products are not necessary and, all by themselves, won't make a complete diet.

"A dog need never ever see a chunk of meat in a lifetime," said Bernard Wasserman, D.V.M., a prominent local veterinarian who has raised many dogs on dry food alone.

Dr. Albert Jonas, director of the Animal Care Division of the Yale School of Medicine, concurs. His laboratories maintain anywhere from 100 to 200 dogs at any give time on dry food.

But at home, Dr. Jonas admitted his Cairn terrier often chomps into a plate of leftovers ("It's a pet. You know, the children.."). Like many lay dog owners, Dr. Jonas has allowed his dog to taste the poorly balanced but more delicious (for dogs as well as people) delights of natural food.

There is no turning back from this. Once a dog has tried real meat from his master's table or meat from a can of dog food, he will probably never be satisfied with the nutritionally splendid boredom of that coarsely ground meal called kibble again.

And so, though he calls an all-leftover diet "bad news" and even turns up his nose at the very popular (with dogs and masters) all-meat dog foods such as Alpo, Dr. Wasserman recommends a compromise diet of dry food supplemented with meat to promote canine appetite and soothe human guilt.

Mrs. Pat O'Keefe, a spokesman for the industry-sponsored Pet Food Institute in Chicago, said she does not think this enthusiasm for dry food was well-founded. She was quick to point to more palatable semimoist and canned foods that are also complete and balanced foods, according to the guidelines laid down by the National Research Council publication, "Nutrient Requirements of the Dog."

Neither Dr. Jonas nor Dr. Wasserman was dogmatically opposed to nondry foods. But they may be reacting to a powerful trend among dog-owners toward buying unbalanced but very palatable products such as 100 per cent horsemeat.

At any rate, much of the mystery of dog food buying for the layman is in the process of disappearing. Already stringent labeling rules are now compelling manufacturers to indicate in plain language which foods are complete and which are supplementary.

But there will always be the problem of taste and connoisseurship. Both dogs and masters will always play an important role in deciding what Fido gets for dinner.

In order, therefore, to survey at least part of the vast current market in dog foods, one 4-year old Saluki bitch and one 31-year-old male food editor both sampled 11 kinds of dog food. Neither subject had eaten 16 hours prior to the experiment; both had been previously corrupted by frequent exposure over long periods of time to a wide variety of meats and meat by-products.

The Saluki, known to her friends as Cleo, point-blank refused to touch dry food—either Gaines Meal or Purina Dog Chow—although she was served it first.

On the other hand, it was a matter of some peril to interrupt her ravenous feasting on the other nine varieties, which ran the gamut from raw ground beef chuck to chicken flavored Prime to Milk-bone biscuit to Top Choice chopped burger to Alpo horsemeat and meat by-products to liver-flavored Daily All-Breed Dog Food.

Cleo ate all the nondry food (and the biscuit) with equal ardor and then took a brief nap. Meanwhile, the food editor tasted small amounts of the same foods, jotted down his reactions and attempted to rate their taste by assigning a theoretically possible four stars to dog food that could be compared to ordinary human food, and so on down to no stars for muck that would make you retch. The stars had nothing to do with nutrition.

His enthusiasm nowhere approached Cleo's, but he did approve the ground chuck and found the Milk-bone tasty enough to consume two biscuits, the second spread with butter. The two foods were the only ones to earn as many as three of the four stars.

Just below these in his estimation came chicken-flavored Prime, which actually bore a surprising resemblance to sweet Passover cake.

There was no disagreement with Cleo about the two dry foods. But Purina Dog Chow was somewhat more palatable than Gaines Meal.

Sometimes an appealing stew odor belied a lack of taste. This was the case with Recipe's beef and egg dinner with vegetables and with Laddie Boy's chunks made with lamb. And both had a texture nigh unto that of cold cream.

The foods with the most unpleasant taste were the Top Choice chopped burger and Alpo horsemeat. One that could not be rated was liver-flavor Daily, an inexpensive homogenized food, brown-green in color and similar in effect to ipecac. It was not rated because it was impossible to force the human subject to taste it. The dog, however, did like it.

☆ ☆ ☆ *Ground chuck.* Needs seasoning.

☆ ☆ ☆ *Milk-Bone Biscuit.* Could replace Ry-Krisp with a little salt and butter.

☆☆ *Prime, chicken-flavored.* No chicken taste; moist, sweet cubes like yellow cake.

☆☆ *Medallion, beef-flavored chunks.* Texture like cake, a strong meat flavor.

☆ *Purina Dog Chow.* Stale biscuit texture, but subtle meat flavor; not appreciably dry when moistened.

☆ *Recipe, beef and egg dinner.* Excellent odor, like chop suey; mushy texture and no seasoning.

☆ *Laddie Boy, lamb chunks.* Best odor of all moist foods, but no taste, gooey texture.

Top Choice, chopped burger. Tasteless, rubbery, drastically red color, pasty in mouth.

Gaines Meal. Like concretized sawdust.

Alpo Horsemeat Chunks. Awful-looking, smelled like stew, tasted foul.

UNRATED

Daily All-Breed, liver flavor. Strong, mysterious odor, couldn't get it down.

Miscellanea

The more I see of men, the better I like my dog.

Frederick the Great

The man who said that the more he saw of mankind, the more he liked his dog, was some species of informer or handman's labourer, that his own mother would run away from, could she but lose him in a big enough crowd.

Brendan Behan

A living dog is better than a dead lion.

Ecclesiastes. IX. 4

The dog commends himself to our favor by affording play to our propensity for mastery, and as he is also an item of expense, and commonly serves no industrial purpose, he holds a well-assured place in men's regard as a thing of good repute.

Thorstein Veblen

To his dog, every man is Napoleon, hence the popularity of dogs.

Anon.

Watson: Is there any point to which you would wish
          to draw my attention?
Holmes: To the curious incident of the dog in the
          night-time.
Watson: The dog did nothing in the night-time.
Holmes: That was the curious incident.

Sir Arthur Conan Doyle

A un perro con dinero lo llaman "Señor Perro."

Spanish proverb

They say a reasonable amount o' fleas is good fer a dog—keeps him from broodin' over bein' a dog, mebbe.

Edward N. Westcott

But was there ever a dog that praised his fleas?

William Butler Yeats

Newfoundland dogs are good to save children from drowning, but you must have a pond of water handy and a child, or else there will be no profit in boarding a Newfoundland.

Josh Billings

Don't let's go to the dogs tonight,
For mother will be there.

Alan P. Herbert

If a dog's prayers were answered, bones would rain from the sky.

Proverb

You ask of my companions. Hills, sir, and the sundown, and a dog as large as myself that my father bought me. They are better than beings, because they know, but do not tell.

Emily Dickinson

Index

Acknowledgments

Text Acknowledgments

We gratefully acknowledge permission to reprint the following copyright material.

Rupert Brooke: *The Little Dog's Day*. Reprinted by permission of Dodd, Mead & Company, Inc. from The Collected Poems of Rupert Brooke. Copyright 1915 by Dodd, Mead & Company. Copyright renewed 1943 by Edward Marsh.

Mikhail Bulgakov: *Heart of a Dog* (Excerpts). Reprinted by permission Grove Press, Inc. Copyright © 1967 by Grove Press, Inc.

Frank Debenham: *Stareek, a Sledge Dog*. By permission of Polar Record, Cambridge, England.

Gerald Carson: *The Most Celebrated Dog Case Ever Tried in Johnson County, Missouri—Or the World*. Copyright 1969 by Gerald Carson. Reprinted by permission of Curtis-Brown Ltd.

Corey Ford: Every Dog Should Own a Man. Reprinted by permission of Harold Ober Associates. Copyright 1952 by Corey Ford.

Jeroslav Hasek: From *The Good Soldier Schweik* by Jeroslav Hasek, translated by Paul Selver. Copyright 1930 by Doubleday & Company, Inc. Reprinted by permission of Doubleday & Company, Inc.

James Herriot: *All Creatures Great and Small* (Excerpt). By permission St. Martin's Press, Inc.

W. H. Hudson: *Dandy*, from *A Traveller in Little Things*. Copyright 1948 by E. P. Dutton & Co. By permission of E. P. Dutton.

Juan Remón Jiménez: *Platero and I* (Excerpt). Translated by Eloise Roach. Copyright 1957. By permission University of Texas Press.

Eric Knight: Copyright 1938 by The Curtis Publishing Company. Copyright renewed ©1966 by Jere Knight, Betty Noyes Knight, Wilfred Knight Mewborn, and Jennie Knight Moore. Reprinted by permission of Curtis-Brown Ltd.

Ring Lardner: Reprinted from *First to Last* by Ring Lardner. Copyright 1934 Ellis A. Lardner. With permission of Charles Scribner's Sons.

Konrad Lorenz: From *Man Meets Dog*. Copyright © 1953. Reprinted by permission of Houghton Mifflin Company.

Dorothy Parker: From The Portable Dorothy Parker. Copyright 1924, 1952 by Dorothy Parker. Reprinted by permission of The Viking Press.

Raymond Sokolov: *Man Bites Dog Foods and Finds Some Are to His Liking*. Copyright 1972 by The New York Times Company. Reprinted by permission.

John Steinbeck: From *Travels with Charley* by John Steinbeck. Copyright 1961, 1962 by The Curtis Publishing Company Inc. Copyright 1962 by John Steinbeck. Reprinted by permission of Viking Press.

James Thurber: *The Scotty Who Knew Too Much*. Copyright © 1940 James Thurber. Copyright 1968 Helen Thurber. From *Fables for Our Time*, published by Harper & Row. Originally printed in *The New Yorker. The Dog That Bit People*. Copyright © 1933, 1961 James Thurber. From *My Life and Hard Times*, published by Harper & Row. *The Story of Barge*. Copyright 1955 James Thurber. From *An Introduction* in *Thurber's Dogs*, published by Simon & Schuster.

Mark Twain: *Uncle Lem's Composite Dog*. Copyright 1922 by Harper & Row, Publishers, Inc. By permission of the publishers.

Hugh Walpole: Reprinted from *All Soul's Night* by Hugh Walpole, copyright 1933. Estate of Hugh Walpole.

E. B. White: Copyright 1941 by E. B. White from *One Man's Meat* by E. B. White.

Art Acknowledgments

We gratefully acknowledge permission to reproduce the following material.

James Henry Beard (American, 1812-1893) *Canine Companions*. Oil on canvas. Courtesy of Berry-Hill Galleries, Inc., New York, N.Y. Page 43.

William Hogarth (1697-1764) *The Painter and His Pug*. The Tate Gallery, London. Photograph by John Webb. Page 9.

Ammi Phillips, Untitled, circa 1855. Collection of Allan L. Daniel. Back Cover.

Henri de Toulouse-Lautrec (1864-1901) *Follette*. Philadelphia Museum of Art: Bequest of Lisa Norris Elkins. Page 1.

Velasquez (1599-1660) *Don Antonio el Inglés*. Museo del Prado, Madrid. Page 59.

Yi Om, 17th Century (Korean, Li Dynasty) *Puppy Carrying Feather*. Watercolor on Silk. Philadelphia Museum of Art. Page 2-3.